The Power of Community-Centered Education

Teaching as a Craft of Place

Michael L. Umphrey

Rowman & Littlefield Education
Lanham, Maryland • Toronto • Plymouth, UK
2007

Published in the United States of America
by Rowman & Littlefield Education
A Division of Rowman & Littlefield Publishers, Inc.
A wholly owned subsidiary of The Rowman & Littlefield Publishing Group,
Inc.
4501 Forbes Boulevard, Suite 200, Lanham, Maryland 20706
www.rowmaneducation.com

Estover Road
Plymouth PL6 7PY
United Kingdom

British Library Cataloguing in Publication Information Available

Library of Congress Cataloging-in-Publication Data

Umphrey, Michael L., 1952–
  The power of community-centered education : teaching as a craft of place /
Michael L. Umphrey.
      p. cm.
  Includes bibliographical references.
  ISBN-13: 978-1-57886-650-2 (hardback : alk. paper)
  ISBN-10: 1-57886-650-2 (hardback : alk. paper)
  ISBN-13: 978-1-57886-651-9 (pbk. : alk. paper)
  ISBN-10: 1-57886-651-0 (pbk. : alk. paper)
  1. Place-based education—Montana. 2. Education, Secondary—Social
aspects—Montana. 3. Montana Heritage Project. I. Title.
  LC239.U66 2007
  370.11'5—dc22
                                                        2007016998

Contents

Foreword

CNN describes the national news of 1995 as "tragic, frustrating, shocking and addictive."[1] That year, the top news stories were the tragic bombing in Oklahoma City and the shocking verdict in the O. J. Simpson trial, after an addictive fascination in the trial itself. At the same time, in a quiet corner of America, an unreported revolution was being forged. The Montana Heritage Project was created with little fanfare and much faith by a consortium of visionary individuals and innovative organizations. The mission of this revolution was to redefine education as we knew it. The aim was to truly make a difference in the lives of students and in their home communities through interpersonal relationships that required concentrated listening and learning. *The Power of Community-Centered Education* is the story of this shockingly simple idea that envisions a place-based educational model that holds enormous promise for educators and students everywhere.

The Montana Heritage Project (MHP) is a partnership of the Library of Congress American Folklife Center (AFC) and a consortium of Montana organizations: the Office of Public Instruction, the University of Montana, Montana State University, the Montana Historical Society, the Montana State Library, the Montana Center for the Book, the Montana Arts Council, and the Montana Committee on the Humanities. The project is the creation of several dedicated individuals: Liz Claiborne and Art Ortenberg, with their generous funding and visionary zeal; Alan Jabbour, then director of the AFC and author of the first proposal; Katherine Mitchell and Marcella Sherfy, the staff of the MHP who are themselves dedicated historians and educators; and finally, Michael

Umphrey, the director of the project, and the person most responsible for its success.

Michael Umphrey was hired to be the founding director of the Montana Heritage Project with a grant from the Liz Claiborne and Art Ortenberg Foundation. With just seed money and a grand vision, Umphrey created an outstanding educational program that has become a national model for school and community collaboration. It was Michael Umphrey who had the energy and intellect to give the project its overall vision and goals, but more important, he was able to skillfully implement them. His attention to both the "big picture" and the myriad, complex details was essential to the creation of the Montana Heritage Project. His most enduring accomplishment is the outstanding staff and the network of dedicated educators that he assembled and retained over the years.

The American Folklife Center at the Library of Congress has been a partner in the Montana Heritage Project since its inception. As folklorists, the staff members of the AFC are trained in the techniques of ethnography and documentation of everyday lives. This work is central to the work of the teachers and students of Montana who are part of the project. By connecting students with community members in the construction of the history, heritage, and folklore of their particular place on earth, the Montana Heritage Project has modeled an educational breakthrough for our times.

From my vantage point in Washington, D.C., where real education reform is often sought and often missed, the Montana model is a standout. The connection between rural Montana schools and the Library of Congress has been exciting and productive. It's an interesting relationship. The Library of Congress is the world's largest repository of knowledge, with a mission "to sustain and preserve a universal collection of knowledge and creativity for future generations." It is fitting that the library should be at the forefront of innovations in education, and thus, we have kept an interest in the Montana Heritage Project at each stage of its development. Michael Umphrey and the educators and young people of the project have been on the front lines of a new sense of purpose for the library, helping us think through what we should be doing for K-12 education as we enter the twenty-first century.

Great libraries are more than collections of books; they are busy community of scholars and researchers. Through the Montana Heritage Program's pioneering work of gathering and interpreting the history and folklife of rural towns and families and sharing that information with the Library of Congress, high school students have demonstrated their ability to join with communities of renowned researchers that have formed around this revered scholarly institution. The road to this pinnacle of scholarship is firmly based in local learning and the relationships that are forged between generations. In this model, everyone is at once a student and a teacher, and lifelong learning is not a concept, but a way of life.

Why the partnership with the American Folklife Center? The study of folklife is the study of how community life and values are expressed through our living libraries—our elders. The concept of giving students a real assignment that requires them to be inventive, to be in conversation with their elders, to be analytical, and finally to produce real results that contribute to the community is one that is based on traditional learning, and it works. It has been observed that 90 percent of our knowledge is folklore (learned by experience), and this is the knowledge that we will pass on to the next generation. Unfortunately, our educational curricula, testing requirements, and bureaucratic busywork have kept teachers and students in a knowledge-restricting straight jacket. *The Power of Community-Centered Education* gives us a blueprint for breaking out of these constraints to give teachers and students a way back to real experience-based, community-centered learning.

The story of America is much richer and deeper than the chronology of political and military events that comprise the historic record. Through the work outlined in *The Power of Community-Centered Education*, we have a road map to experience a profound sense of place and a deep knowledge of our own belonging by focusing on the places where we live. We learn how our own communities formed, how they preserve local knowledge, how students and teachers can use primary documents to get a firsthand grasp of history, and how community knowledge shapes what America will remember.

Community-centered education is not only a powerful pedagogy, but it also offers students an opportunity to contribute important scholarship that will live on well into the future. If you visit the Library of Congress today and want to find information about Montana community life or oral history—including the folklife and community history of Roundup, Chester, Libby, Corvallis, Simms, or Townsend—you will find that the primary research and documentary materials in the collections are the product of high school students who participated in the Montana Heritage Project. These documents are valuable to the historic record and are part of our archival holdings that will be used by scholars in the coming decades. It has been exciting to recognize the undeniable talents and creativity of teenagers who are documenting, interpreting, and preserving the unique and special experiences and knowledge of people living in small towns in the American West. This is a model to replicate across the nation—giving important work to our next generation of citizens while they are still forming their values and worldviews.

In October 2000 the U.S. Congress passed Public Law 106-380 that created the Veterans History Project (VHP) at the American Folklife Center. The VHP is now the largest oral history collection in the United States, with over 45,000 interviews and more arriving each day. The students of the Montana Heritage Project have been involved in this congressionally mandated work since its inception. Our experience is that teenagers are the best documentarians of our veterans—especially the Grand Generation. The work outlined in *The Power of Community-Centered Education* is exactly fitted to the work that is required for the Veterans History Project, where powerful insights and community connections are made when young people learn firsthand about service and sacrifice in a time well past. These insights are captured in the words of Claire Stanfill, written when she was a junior at Bigfork High School:

> How do you survive a tour of duty in a war zone and maintain a marriage while you and your wife are living in two worlds that are as different as one can imagine? How do you support your relationship and remain in contact in a world that does not have e-mail, instant messaging, text messages, video conferencing, cell or satellite phones? Bob Reed, a career Marine Corps officer, chose to use the time-honored means that men at war have used for centuries: the letter. Bob wrote hundreds of letters to his wife, Virginia, during his tours overseas.

Our Bigfork High School Montana Heritage Project received a remarkable gift that would open a whole new avenue for understanding communication between those on the front lines and their loved ones left behind. Ginny Reed brought us a Nike shoebox containing over two hundred letters that her husband Bob had written to her while he was serving in the Marine Corps during the 1960s. Reading the letters in that box seemed like a daunting task but one that could reveal how spouses and families manage long, lonely periods of separation while their loved ones are at war.[2]

The partnerships between community members and students, such as the one described above, facilitate education while at the same time they create intergenerational bonds that nourish the community itself. This is the beauty of place-based pedagogy.

The Power of Community-Centered Education is a passionate and personal testimonial based on real experiences in education. This book should be a "must" for all adults who are educating children and young adults; in fact, it's a book for all of us. Umphrey's experiences as the director of the Montana Heritage Project for the past twelve years have resulted in a unique and important view of the way that we learn, and the way that we construct our lives from this learning.

—Peggy A. Bulger

NOTES

1. CNN Year in Review, www.cnn.com/EVENTS/year_in_review/index.html.

2. Claire Stanfill, Their legacy living on through letters, Heritage Online, www.montanaheritageproject.org/index.php/home/their-legacy-living-through-letters.

Introduction

When I came onboard as the newly hired director of the Montana Heritage Project, the project amounted to little more than a gathering of bureaucrats around a heap of money. It was a new program initiated by the Library of Congress, and according to the proposal funded by the Liz Claiborne and Art Ortenberg Foundation, the project was supposed to have something to do with cultural heritage and authentic research. I had recently resigned from my job as a high school principal, and I thought I saw in the project an open field where I might try some ideas about teaching and learning that had been a long time forming.

Ten years into the project, we were endorsed by then–U.S. secretary of education Richard Riley and held up as a model for the nation by Librarian of Congress James Billington. More interestingly, we had testimonials from thousands of students and dozens of teachers and parents that something new and important was happening at school.

What was happening, of course, was that students were excited by the scholarly research they were doing—they talked about their school work with the sort of enthusiasm more commonly elicited by athletic contests. The big institutions that had signed on to the project—nearly all the important cultural agencies in the state—in truth did little but provide an appreciative audience for the work the teachers set in motion and the students accomplished. Early on we all came to count on serendipity, trusting that what we needed would come. We learned that serendipity is a normal occurrence among people who have decided to go where others wish there was a way.

For one thing, the project attracted staff who wanted something more than a job. There was Marcella Sherfy, who had served as the state's historic preservation officer and had contacts everywhere, along with a reputation for doing the right things and seeing that necessary tasks got finished. Her work led to broad knowledge of local heritage, particularly how history's stories could be read in the built environment of a downtown business district or a remote farmstead. She provided us with instant credibility when she joined the project as our education director. "She's a research machine," one sophomore noted in awe after spending an afternoon with her at the Montana Historical Society archives. She taught students advanced research skills in primary documents in their local courthouses and in the state archives and she showed them how to form questions and strategies for finding answers by examining the traces of history that are visible on every main street.

It was not a minor blessing that she was married to Dave Walter, one of Montana's premiere research historians. He loved the project and gave many hours of time to training teachers and teaching students. He took pleasure in the way the project linked two things he cared about deeply: young people and Montana's history. When, during the first year of the project, this noted author praised the first collection of research-based writings that came in—from high school juniors in Renee Rasmussen's English classes in Chester—our start-up jitters calmed a bit. Walter said, "these students not only gathered the history of Chester's buildings, they skillfully told the stories that put real people in those buildings."

The telling of the stories was largely the province of Katherine Mitchell, our editor and writing coach for teachers and students throughout the state. She helped get masses of information into clear and vivid language. We all knew that to get where we wanted to go we needed to create our own paths, and that to do that we would need to tell our own stories. Teaching writing is maybe the hardest challenge in schools, and Katherine's skill and patience was crucial in teaching what needed to be learned.

We were also lucky in our institutional affiliations. At the Liz Claiborne and Art Ortenberg Foundation, Liz and Art themselves took a very personal interest in the development of the project, which made things happen that otherwise never would have happened. Affiliation with a prestigious foundation whose principals were available and accessible mattered enormously. Those who lead schools and other government agencies often respond more readily to the charms of money and proximity to fame than they do to the most clear and compelling of reasons. I found this to be more true than I would have liked. Art and Liz understood this and many other things, and they were willing to put themselves out repeatedly to advance the cause. Every year they flew from New York to Helena to attend the Youth Heritage Festival, our academic conference where high school students reported on their research to their peers and to an audience as large and as important as we could get. Art and Liz's presence helped get the governor, the superintendent of public instruction, and other VIPs to attend. This, in turn, helped make believers of the kids when we told them the work they were doing was important. It was something of a conspiracy, and Art and Liz were the leading conspirators. A few thousand kids owe them thanks.

Besides Liz and Art, we had the prestige of the Library of Congress. Alan Jabbour and then later Peggy Bulger, directors of the American Folklife Center, came to our events regularly. Jim Billington, the Librarian of Congress, came one year. He spent a couple days dodging important people who wanted audiences and interviews so he could visit with high school scholars from little towns on the Northern Great Plains.

All in all, it was the most pleasant conspiracy I've ever been part of—a conspiracy to surround young people with a narrative environment that told them, repeatedly and in many forms, that by learning to research and write well enough to tell the stories of their own people in a compelling way, they were doing a heroic work, saving histories that otherwise would vanish. Surrounded by such a conspiracy, how could the kids doubt it? And believing it, they made it true. It *was* true because so many believed it and acted on behalf of it. The kids really did learn to research and write well. It really was important work that changed those who were part of it.

Of course, the conspiracy would have amounted to little without that exquisite sort of drudgery through which classroom teachers connect the unruly energy of young minds with the records and transcripts of all that's gone before. From the beginning the project attracted experienced and skilled teachers who were still looking for better ways to do their work—teachers whose steady optimism had become a form of character. The first year, Renee Rasmussen in the northern plains farming community of Chester set her students out studying the history of their town by researching in courthouse records and by oral interviews the histories of various buildings; Marta Brooks sent her students on the Flathead Reservation in search of the various ways farmers, Native Americans, and sportsmen thought about rivers; and Jeff Gruber in Libby had his senior civics students invite a dozen of the community's leaders to work with them on a twelve-week investigation of the most pressing concerns faced by a logging community going through economic and environmental disruptions. Again and again teachers turned the abstract and lofty language of grant proposals into completed student projects that were hard to argue with.

Since the schools existed in different communities with different histories, different community agencies, and different people, the projects took different forms in each place. Our guidelines for teachers were simple. We wanted them to create heritage projects—scholarly research projects worthy of being placed in local archives as a legacy to future researchers. Each heritage project needed to pose broad and important questions; each needed to involve the students in original research; and each needed to result in a tangible intellectual product.

The questions we talked about most those first years were: "What does it take to build community?" and "What does it take to sustain community?" The very asking of such questions attracted teachers who were interested in conversations about the relationships between people and places. Many of those teachers turned out to have substantial expertise in what it means to be a member of a community, as well as considerable ingenuity in crafting teaching units that relied less on slick commercial materials than on the photographs and records to be found in family photo albums, courthouse file cabinets, and museum archives.

The project also attracted community members such as Chuck Merja in the Sun River Valley, a Stanford-trained engineer, who assisted students in ambitious digital mapping projects, and Paul Rumelhart, a Libby businessman and philosopher, who spent hours at meetings with teenagers, researching the town's past and making recommendations for its future. Our experience confirmed that the teaching passion is natural to people and broadly distributed through our neighborhoods and towns.

The main attraction for all these people was, of course, the students themselves. Again and again our young people confirmed our belief that when we demonstrate the value we place on our humanity by listening to ordinary people, recording their stories, and researching their histories, the kids will figure out, correctly, that we are placing a great value on *them*. We elevate the importance and dignity of the work they do in school. We link their schoolwork both to identity formation and to reality—but maybe "link" is too puny a word. Identity and reality are—like school and culture—not things but activities. When we get it right, we learn by creating ourselves—not out of nothing but out of the places we, literally, find ourselves, the cultural and material nexus that shapes us, limits us, and entices us to contemplate a thousand horizons.

Everyone knows that to be an adolescent is to be tangled up in the work of forming identity. Erik Erickson's work on the stages we go through in life has been so influential that his phrase "identity crisis" has entered the popular consciousness as a basic feature of how we understand adolescence. Later work, most notably by Dan McAdams (1988), made clear the extent to which identity has a narrative basis. Though we might answer the question, "what am I?" in many ways— I am an organism; I am an electro-chemical system; I am an accountant; I am Irish—to the question "who am I?" the answer has to be, "I am the one to whom these things have happened—the person who did and said these things. I am this particular story.

McAdams says that "identity is a life story which individuals begin constructing, consciously and unconsciously, in late adolescence." We can't think of our identity apart from the work of authoring our life story. We are our story.

Another important insight follows quite naturally: identities, like other stories, have genres. Hamlet couldn't really be Hamlet if his story ended in a comic farce. Carol Pearson (1989) says most of us make our life stories fit one of the six narrative forms we learn growing up (she calls them archetypes): the Innocent, the Orphan, the Wanderer, the Warrior, the Martyr, and the Magician. Researchers among elderly people in Scandinavia (Ruth and Oberg, 1996) decided that most of their subjects could be classified according to what story they thought they were living: the Suffering One, the Loser, the Fighter, the Altruist, the Careerist, or the Happy One.

No such list is exhaustive, of course. Our own cultural tool kits might include genres that help us see ourselves as tricksters, disciples, or knights. The important point, for now, is that the genres aren't inborn. Students learn them from the narrative environments that surround them. Blessed is the child born to a family woven of happy stories. Fortunately, identities can be revised and new genres can be learned. In fact, such learning is a necessity of living a human life. Since each young person's life story is unique, requiring original authorship, to live well they need to develop narrative intelligence.

This means they need to learn to emplot, finding useful stories in the rush of episodes and events which besiege every conscious mind. This often means they must discern or decide where things are going and select which details are pertinent—part of the story—and which are not. They need to learn to recognize patterns and find themes. Meanings aren't attached like price tags to the events of daily life. It's not even always clear what is an event and what is merely motion. Meaning is to a great extent a "roll your own" kind of deal. And yet it is death to live without it or to try to get by with interpretations so wrong or weak that we can't grow with the dislocations that surely come or that don't help us civilize the wild forces whirling up within us.

For young people, the challenge is often to revise their life stories for unity and coherence. Anyone who works with teenagers sees that many of them have trouble making coherent stories of themselves, but without coherence they can't form or execute sensible plans.

Where are young people to learn such things—to emplot their lives, to tune their identities to chosen themes? They learn them from us. We provide this help by paying conscious attention to their narrative environment, by weaving and shaping that environment. For teenagers, the narrative environment is the tool kit with which they find the roles and scripts they need to live.

My hunch is that educators in our day are fated to pay increasing attention to the narrative environment as bad stories in our midst drive home to us the importance of stories. In traditional societies, the narrative environment was largely a given in a way that it may never be again. We have lost our innocence. It becomes increasingly clear that the worst troubles our youth face are caused by their entanglement in bad stories. Though we set up metal detectors at every school door, these won't detect or deter narrative contagions moving through us.

Over the past few decades the scholarly basis for increased attention to the narrative environment has been well established. Researchers such as Theodore Sarbin (1986) and David Hermans (2002) tell us that adolescents increasingly internalize their narrative environment. Russian psychologist Lev Vygotsky (1988) shows how the voices young people hear around them gradually become the voices they hear inside themselves, so that as adults, they experience thought as a conversation, having incorporated voices from the narrative environment into their own psychology. Lucky kids internalize the cheerful, friendly, and useful voices of family, friends, and good literature, but one needn't be overly perceptive watching young moviegoers adopt the swagger, catchphrases, and fashion sense of Hollywood stars to see that their identities can also be shaped by other storytellers. Parents have always had to guard their kids from the rough stories one could hear in the taverns and hangouts miscreants have always formed on the outskirts of respectable communities, but modern society is notable for lavishly supporting a huge storytelling industry that flourishes in part by propagating tales that exult in attempts to dissolve that society's own cultural foundations. In truth, the narrative product of mass media is often wretched. And it's getting worse—fast. The Internet has enticed many youth into story worlds that are precisely as tawdry and vile as the worst among us can imagine. I suppose that the narrative environment of such youth may not be more toxic than that of unfortunate children who have endured firsthand the barbarities of genocide and wars, but, as Mercutio gasped, "'tis enough, 'twill serve."

According to the Commission on Children at Risk (2003), the culture that surrounds children in America today is poisoning them. The evidence can be seen in rising levels of self-destructive behavior among the children of immigrants. Though "adolescents from immigrant families are less likely than U.S.-born adolescents to experience school absences due to health or emotional problems, and are also *less* likely to report engaging in risky behaviors, from early sex to substance use, delinquency and violence," this advantage fades over time, and, by the third generation, "rates of [risk] behaviors approach those of U.S.-born white adolescents." Their conclusion: "The basic foundations of childhood appear currently to be at best anemic, in the sense of weak and inadequate to foster full human flourishing, and at worst toxic."

The alternative to this toxic culture is—well, culture. An authentic human culture that we make out of the best that is in us. The days are gone when the narrative environment of young people was provided more or less reliably by folk cultures that linked each new generation with ancient traditions that, though they contained infelicities, were also rich in guidance for living that, tested through centuries of experience, helped young people avoid the worst mistakes. Today, every community has kids who take their bearings from a crass commercial culture in which songs and stories often serve no cultural purpose more noble than the enrichment of people who are neither good nor wise. "Sense of place" has become a buzzword because people long to escape life in what seems a thousand miles of strip mall, where all the stories are intended to make you pay. Those concerned with the education of young people can no longer ignore or take for granted the narrative environment.

Our most powerful teachers have always been those who tell the stories that most powerfully influence our emotions. Parents and teachers should not delegate this work, by default, to the Internet or movies or television or music. To teach young people deeply and effectively, we must participate in intentional work at the narrative level. In its most powerful form, this means we must live stories that take kids with us to the heart of what we care for.

It also means that we need to monitor and select the stories that shape young identities, but such prophylactic approaches won't be enough unless we also work with young people to create and tell our own stories. We will find what we most need in our own families and our community's treasury of folkways. The explosion of digital tools and the development of the read-write Web gives us the tools we need to restore culture to its proper place as a community's greatest treasure and most important creation.

And why not? It's what we are meant to do. Like cowboys making up songs around a campfire, we hanker to create the culture we inhabit. We suffer psychic afflictions when we delegate too much of the creative work.

After decades of work across a host of disciplines, it's generally accepted today that stories are powerfully educative, not just as illustrations of this or that homily but as primary constituents of human consciousness. This is as true of bad stories as of good ones. Our work as teachers is made difficult because we live in a society that is increasingly characterized by competing narratives—a society in which no story is so bad that it has no champions. In fact, saying that anything is good or bad invites controversy since one variant of the modern identity is roused to fury at the very idea of goodness. The idea of goodness carries within it those dread possibilities of judgment and shame.

All cultural norms are being challenged. You may have heard that you have no right to impose your values on others. This is often asserted by those intent on imposing their values on everyone, arguing only that whoever doesn't like it can stop listening or go somewhere else. Of course, parents and teachers have the same right to assert their vision of what is good and true as does the avant-garde filmmaker or the corporate marketer with something to peddle. Nietzsche saw that in the nihilistic world that lies beyond good and evil, what's left is power and will. When we meet power and will that care not at all for what we value, a debate is seldom useful. At some point, we simply need to stand for what we stand for.

We can, if we choose, make the question of what makes a good story—or rather, what makes a story good—so complex that we can't answer it. We can split hairs and lose our way in trying to draw lines precise enough to satisfy those who cannot be satisfied because they do not want any lines. Whose stories? they ask, by way of asserting that we haven't the right to talk about what is good. But the important questions about stories have less to do with ownership than with meaning. Stories pass readily through time and across cultural barriers, smuggling their precious cargo into new human hearts. It is the portability of stories that gives them their great power and value. They belong to all who "get" them—their universality affirms our essential humanity and helps us understand our ephemeral differences.

Which stories are good? This is the fundamental question, and educators should not be deterred from asking it and offering their answers. We can trust our sense that stories that affirm life are better than stories that diminish it. We needn't prove that stories that help us understand each other are better than stories that teach us to distrust each other. We don't need studies showing that the lived stories of people restoring a river are better than stories of filling a river with industrial sludge. Good stories help us want to live together and they show us the little secrets that make happiness more likely. They help us see how we can strengthen relationships. The best stories help us understand community, and they enlarge our sense of community to include more people, and more of the natural world. Another way of saying this is that the best stories help us understand the greatest order.

It is through such stories that we educate desire, making our emotions more intelligent, helping us make the places we live more like the places we want to live. There is a kind of place making that is the most civilized and civilizing of pursuits. It is an extension of our gardening urge, turning our attention to whole neighborhoods. If we are going to live in places with museums and libraries and gardened walks and well-tended parks, it will be because we decide to make them that way. If we are going to live in communities that are orderly and peaceful, with healthy people and pristine nature and abundant wildlife, it will because we decide to make them that way.

The main idea of this book is that education and place making are two aspects of the same process. One of life's central purposes is to make the places we live better and it is a purpose that can only be achieved through intelligent communion with reality. Such a communion with reality, supported by such a purpose, gives us a way to think about what education needs to be.

Our pioneering and homesteading great-grandparents and forebears understood better than we sometimes do the way that education and place making are of a piece. They succeed or fail together. It was often the need for education—the pressing need to build schools—that first pulled isolated settlers into community. In Percy Wollaston's memoirs of homesteading in Montana around 1910 (1997), he notes how focused people were on place making. When new people arrived, the conversation quickly turned to the future. What people wanted to know about newcomers was "what each planned to make of his place" and what plans they had "for the future of the community."

Things might seem more challenging today, when most of us live in places that seem overbuilt, amid huge institutions and agencies that run things and that seem far beyond our control. Few of us think a great deal about place making, beyond planting an entry garden or a back-yard tree. But in truth, our need for joining with neighbors in place making has never been greater, though it's not the built environment of roads and buildings that we now lack. What our places sorely lack is an intentional folklife, a narrative environment that gives us places to be listened to and a sense of understanding how we are influencing one another. When we think of our work as cultural place making, we begin to see all sorts of ways people and institutions can be invited into better alignment.

The modern world creates new forms of isolation. We've long been a lonely people, and recent evidence suggests we are getting lonelier (Easterbrook, 2003). We might ask why, in a nation of unprecedented material abundance, do growing numbers of children suffer from depression, addiction, anxiety, suicidal thoughts, and other spiritual and behavioral problems? Can it be that our folklife has become anemic, leaving kids adrift in incoherent bureaucracies where one committee talks about adjusting the curriculum to satisfy abstract standards created afar, while a different committee discusses the five-year plan to improve instruction, and yet other committees make plans to address dropouts or bullying?

Can we pull together into one conversation our talk about what kids need intellectually, emotionally, physically, socially, and spiritually? Such a conversation would not be a narrow affair of interest only to professional educators. Indeed, grownups have always been at their best when they band together out of concern for their young, and more than anything, it is their concern for children that brings adults out of narrow selfishness and into their sanest thoughts about the future. It is preeminently by thinking about what young people need that groups of adults think together productively about place making—about what makes any place a good place to live. Most people still respond when young people come to them in person to ask for help. We don't need to create an ideal community which will then provide everything kids need. Kids, like the rest of us, don't need perfect communities. What they do need is invitations to join the work in progress of making places better. Great nations emerge from great folklife. There is no other way.

The work of civic renewal can't be separated from the work of education. Indeed, to a great extent the work of civic renewal will always be the work of education. The future of democracy cannot be secured except through education, and the work of educating young people is accomplished through attention to folkways. The bedrock meaning of freedom is realized in the lives of families and neighborhoods.

Education for young people is, now as always, local work. Large institutions can lend their prestige, but if they do too much, they risk setting things back by further eroding the attractions of community and local responsibility that are needed. But one teacher in one community who takes students into a community as hunter-gatherers, as explorers with questions, as friends and neighbors, as participants with a mission sets in motion the forces of an educational renaissance. Such work is a gift taking the form of an invitation. It starts a story.

In a poorer past, only emperors and warriors and kings were considered worthy of literature. But thanks to writers such as Dickens and Tolstoy, we learned the value of ordinary lives. And thanks to modern wealth and the ease of digital publishing, it's now possible for every family and town to create its own literature. Indeed, it's nearly impossible not to. The important questions have to do only with the quality of a literature that most assuredly we will create.

It's a cultural imperative that today's young people learn to observe and take notes well, because they are making the first drafts of what will be our culture. They need direct encounters with nature, with historic sites, and with people who do and have done real work. They need to collect, analyze, and interpret information, and they need to learn how to speak with honesty and intelligence. They need to develop their personal voices, backed by research and made bold by attentive audiences.

Our future will be shaped less and less by twentieth-century media such as NBC and more and more by emerging forums such as MySpace and YouTube. The question we now face is not whether our youth will create their own culture with the tools they are acquiring. The question is only how good the culture they create will be. Will it support the development of that integrity which is our most fully human defense against the dissolutions of nature and time? Will it make a story they will want to tell years and years from now? Will it be true to enduring principles?

Having lost our innocence, it's important that we do not lose our courage and our capacity for self-renewal. Our young people need us to tell them they are part of our story and we are part of their story and we wouldn't have it any other way. It's a great story, and, like stories of neighbors working together to build a barn, enjoying the smell of fresh-hewn pine at first light and enjoying supper with friends as the sun wanes, it's a story full of grace. It will have a happy ending because it contains moments that have no end.

CHAPTER 1

Crisis in the Narrative Environment

Because schools are ritual centers cut off from the real living places where we love and hate, we burden them with all the elaborate aspirations that our love and labor are too meager and narrow to bear.

—Madeline Grumet

DISENGAGEMENT

Rose Goyen invited me to Libby to teach a unit on writing the "essay of place" to her high school juniors. Rose was herself a gifted teacher, with an Irish smile in her eyes and a penchant for story in her voice. Former students raved about her willingness to hear what they were trying to say in their writing and about the insistently kind ways she led and pushed them to say it more clearly. So I felt a little pressure.

She introduced me as a poet with two published books, and I hoped my "credentials" might buy me time to get warmed up. My work as director of the Montana Heritage Project had kept me off the teaching frontline for the past few years, and I felt out of shape.

But no luck. The kids from Libby weren't impressed by credentials. Libby had always been a tough logging town, and it hadn't softened in the hard times that followed when the mills shut down. Amid the stunning beauty of the Cabinet Mountains, it was often a hard place to live. Montana has always attracted dreamers, and Montana's history was rich with stories of fantasies and theories put to the test and found wanting. Abandoned homesteads—graying testaments to failed dreams—can be seen on nearly any back road. Ghost towns still cling to mountain ridges where people came to get rich and stayed only till the lode played out. Like many other places, Libby has been hard hit. It was built around logging and mining, but the mills and mines are gone. What remains is a world-famous superfund site along with high mortality rates from asbestosis and mesothelioma. It's a community that has been, seemingly forever, trying to figure out what comes next. Some of the kids had inherited a cultural distrust of knowledge that sounded too bookish, or that hadn't been earned on the tricky slopes of lived experience.

I was ten minutes into my spiel when a big kid in a blue flannel shirt and frayed Levis who could have used a shave stopped me. "This is boring," he announced, cutting me off in mid-sentence, staring defiantly from his seat in the middle of the room.

I stopped and looked back. He didn't flinch or waver. As far as he was concerned, we were equals. He had as much right to be there with his opinion as I did with mine. It made me laugh out loud, restoring me instantly to familiar terrain—the eternal classroom struggle. Me, the old guy with plans, and him, the young guy with, well, other plans. I tumbled somewhat unceremoniously out of whatever blue sky I had imagined onto the comfortable ground of ordinary talk.

"What's your name?" I asked him.

"Todd."

"Todd, your responsibility whenever things get boring is to think of something interesting to tell us."

Think of something interesting. That was the real work. We all have interests, of course, and what we find interesting is information that touches upon those interests. The trouble with schooling is that many young people do not see how the curriculum that we so dutifully deliver touches upon their interests. Lots of studies have confirmed that disengagement from school is epidemic among students from all social, economic, and academic levels. In one large-scale (twenty thousand teenagers in nine American communities), long-term (two years of pilot testing, four years of data collection, and four years of data analysis) research project by a team of social scientists from Stanford University, Temple University, and the University of Wisconsin, the conclusion reported by Laurence Steinberg (1996) was that student disengagement from learning is the most serious problem we face.

"The picture that emerged from our research was disheartening—alarmingly so," notes Steinberg. "Indeed, I came away from the study feeling that the problems facing our country's educational system—and consequently, our country itself—are deep, pervasive, and profound. In real life, as on television, America's students are largely disengaged from the serious business of education."

Steinberg points out that "the widespread disengagement of America's students is a problem with enormous implications and profound potential consequences." Many of our other problems stem from or are aggravated by this problem. "Although it is less visible, less dramatic, and less commented upon than other social problems involving youth—crime, pregnancy, violence—student disengagement is more pervasive and some ways potentially more harmful to the future well-being of American society."

A few decades ago students who were uninterested in school either dropped out or were kicked out. Today, great efforts are made to see that most students get high school diplomas. This has led to "extraordinary changes . . . in American schools in the past twenty-five years" due to "the shift in the relative proportions of engaged and disengaged students." Steinberg notes that "teachers have always encountered students who were difficult to interest and hard to motivate, but the number of these students was considerably smaller in the past than it is today. Two decades ago, a teacher in an average high school in this country could expect to have three or four 'difficult' students in a class of thirty. Today, teachers in these same schools are expected to teach to classrooms in which nearly half of the students have 'checked out.'"

The main reason students drop out of high school is that they are disengaged from schooling and they perceive it as boring. Four out of five dropouts say they would have been more likely to finish school if it had been more engaging, more connected to the "real" world.

These are not new insights. William Glasser (1998) argued decades earlier that about half the young people in a typical high school class make no consistent effort to learn. Getting tough with these students tends to be no more effective than threatening a worker who is already looking for a better job. Students, like other living things, do what satisfies them, and they find little payoff in doing schoolwork. Sure, a diploma has value, but that payoff is too far away, and besides, to get more kids to graduate we've made getting a diploma more a matter of attendance than study. Students know they don't need to engage. Some consider studying hard, from time to time, but many are like an overweight boy who would love to be thin but continues eating because the payoff from dieting seems too distant to be felt as real.

THE WORLD OUTSIDE THE WINDOW

To get kids to engage, we need to reengage. The story of how I had come to be in Libby talking about essays that delved into the history and ecology of local places was a story of my own reengagement with schooling. I had resigned as a high school principal some years before, after a new superintendent abruptly undid several years of restructuring, leaving me with the feeling that I was wasting my time. I'd thought a good school would be like a cultivated landscape where making the place better day by day would be as natural as, well, gardening. But experience left me feeling that was a quixotic delusion. Was it possible to turn a politically governed bureaucracy into a place where it felt natural to invest one's best efforts in making things better?

The school was troubled when I was hired. The student disengagement was in part a response to teacher disengagement. There was the English teacher who passed the time by having students work on crossword puzzles while he read the paper. There was the history teacher who had students copy the overhead transparencies he had created decades before. There was the shop teacher who joked he was teaching math skills as he played poker with the kids all afternoon. Of course kids were disengaged. There was an unreality in the place that filled classrooms like the smell of tennis shoes and floor wax.

I could deal with such teachers, one by one, but where were they coming from? Public schools have permeable boundaries. Since school leaders have little say over which teachers or students show up, only very gifted leaders with lots of luck and lots of energy—and with more authority than modern schools often grant—could sustain an intellectual and ethical environment within the school at a higher level than that of the community its participants came in from in the morning and returned to in the evening.

Most troubles that vex schools don't originate in schools. They are manifestations of faltering communities: kids who don't come to school or come with hostility toward school authorities; parents who act on the assumption that any rule that doesn't benefit their child at the moment can have no legitimate public purpose; kids whose attention is dissipated by drugs, money, music, and sex; kids who have learned neither good manners nor such basic work habits as patience, humility, and diligence.

It's our plight that most kids really do learn what their families and communities really do teach. This cuts to the heart of both our dilemma and our hope. If we want our kids to read, we need to be readers. If we want our kids to make music, we need to bring music into their world. If we want our kids to be honest, we are obliged to work on figuring out what the truth is so we can say it. A town that wants its youngsters to be the sort of people who solve complex problems, incorporating the scholarly virtues into their lives by digging for information, withholding opinions while gathering evidence, collaborating with others to get their minds around facts in those difficult ways we call knowing, and being honest about what is known and not known—well, the people of such a town will just have to do likewise. It's an old cliché that we teach who we are. Who would be surprised to learn that the Kennedy family talked politics at the dinner table? It's no accident that politics—as well as medicine and auto racing—tends to run in families.

Much of our trouble stems from the fact that the more distant schools are from the communities where the parents live, the more trouble schools have turning out students who love the things their elders love. Unfortunately, that's not a bad thing by the lights of many educators. I've run into many educators who think that it is precisely their work to transform the world by transforming students into creatures quite different from their parents. In the talk of such educators—"transformative intellectuals"—I think I hear the narrow drone of hornets.

Though there are places where communities and families have so weakened that adolescents are on their own and educators have little choice but to seek a transformation, in most places parents are still present, if somewhat distracted. If teachers believe that the place they have landed is so benighted that they are tempted to separate the kids from their local culture, I would suggest that instead they try to think of the entire community as the unit of educational change. Transforming a society tends be more complex than we think it will be when we start out, and intellectuals don't, unfortunately, have a great track record at doing so directly—that is, by methods other than allowing the insights of scholarship to percolate through the culture. On the other hand, teachers who do engage the community by, for example, doing heritage projects will hear what is known about community by many different members—those who operate the wastewater plants, retired foresters, grandmothers, police officers, road maintenance managers, real estate loan officers, architects, sawmill operators, ambulance attendants, and fishermen with forty-year memories of the local river. This deepens the thinking of all but the most obtuse.

In any case, we aren't likely to make public schools much better than the communities they arise from, so we are going to improve schooling only when we figure out how to bring at least a part of the community, willingly, with us. In practice that may mean one teacher drawing on as many community members and organizations as time and energy permits. Early in the Montana Heritage Project, I listened to a team of Jeff Gruber's students from Libby, Montana, give a presentation they developed with the help of their community to officials at the U.S. Forest Service regional headquarters in Missoula.

Over the years, I've learned a lot from Jeff. When Jeff and another person start talking at once, Jeff is usually the first to stop. He believes in listening, and when he speaks, he's thoughtful. Walking around his hometown, we seldom got far before someone stopped him to fill him in on the news from their part of the community—young mothers, retired foresters, high school students, forest service anthropologists, town council members, hunters, ministers, loggers—he truly lives in his community. He always seems to have time.

His students' presentation in Missoula was sort of a practice run. They had researched a hundred-year environmental history of their place to present to the powers that be at the headquarters of the Stimson Lumber Company and the Plum Creek Lumber Company in Portland. Although Libby was a logging community that had been buffeted by business decisions made by those two companies, the kids did not imagine villains—their game was not blaming but understanding. In that spirit, they wanted the corporate officers to understand the sometimes devastating impact their actions had on the local community. They were beginning to understand that one reason for learning was to find their voice.

I met the team of student researchers in the conference room at the forest service headquarters. Students bustled about setting up their projectors and podiums to read their scripts. Others set up cameras to document the event. Jeff stood off to the side visiting with the forest service archivist, not seeming to pay much attention to the students. They knew what they were doing. It was their show.

Actually, Jeff told me he had resisted pressure from his students to schedule the presentations because the whole thing made him nervous, but the kids insisted that it would not be a problem. Their engagement engaged him. Jeff had resigned as head football coach after his first year of doing heritage projects with kids, so he would have more time for them. They were doing real work.

When the audience was seated and the lights darkened, the students began their show. Using photographs they had gathered from area archives, they presented an environmental history of the valley and the forests where they lived. They began with the Kootenai Indians, talking about how they used fire to modify the ponderosa pine forests to suit their needs better. They showed photographs of trees where strips of bark had been removed a hundred years before, exposing the sugary cambium layer that the Kootenai harvested each spring. They had early photographs of massive deer kills from a period in the nineteenth century when loggers were out of work and turned to hunting and selling hides, thousands of them, to make ends meet.

Working from a carefully researched script, the eight students took turns narrating as slides documented the way land use changed as technology changed from horse skidding, to steam donkeys, to diesel tractors with tracks, to rubber-tired skidders. They brought the history up to the present with photographs they had made of contemporary logging operations, featuring clippers that cost several hundred thousand dollars and allow a single operator to cut a tree, delimb it, saw it to length, and deposit it in a log deck in just a few minutes. They showed the changes as loggers quit using the river to move logs after the railroad came, and then later quit using the railroad when trucks became feasible.

They also followed the changes in land ownership by major corporations, and the ways those corporations responded to the global economy, and the differing attitudes they took toward local communities, and the effects this had on ordinary people.

The students said they had begun their study because they were depressed about the future and thought they might find answers by examining the past. But after researching decades of what seemed to be nonstop economic troubles, the kids concluded their presentation with this insight: "We looked to Libby's past for answers to our current troubles. But we didn't find answers. What we found was that life had always been difficult, but that our grandparents and great-grandparents had always found a way to help each other and to get through hard times. And so will we."

It was a little parable. The kids knew they were facing trouble, but they didn't know what to do or how to feel. So they gathered the stories of their tribe. It wasn't problem solving, exactly—the problem is still there. It was far more important than that. It was *identity forming*. The kids decided that they were the sort of people who face up to hard times, who reach out to family and friends, and who always find a way. The problems in Libby were obvious—closing mills, asbestosis—but the gifts took a bit of work to recognize: the joy of figuring things out and the comfort and even pleasure of handling adversity in the company of friends. Now, they said, they still thought the future was difficult and uncertain, but they were confident they would be able to meet the challenges they would need to meet, just as their parents and grandparents and great-grandparents had.

From the point of view of a writing teacher, I was thrilled that they had come to understand that to speak in a voice strong enough to keep their place, they needed to study. Through researching together they had formed a "we" that included all their classmates but also their parents and grandparents and the other place makers who had created Libby. Seeing themselves as members of this large and durable "we" had given them courage.

By engaging in their own bit of place making, they had strengthened their narrative identities, which is to say that they had found themselves, or constructed themselves if you prefer, by immersing themselves in the particular narrative environment that constituted their home place.

After their presentation, I went to lunch with them at the Country Kitchen just off I-90 on Reserve Street. I asked questions and like all researchers they were pleased to share stories of the obstacles as well as the serendipity they encountered along the way. We examined each other's cameras. Marsha, a blond girl with interested eyes, told me that what she liked most about Jeff's class was the friendships that were formed in the process of doing research. As a team, they visited libraries, interviewed people, and spent time at local archives. Day by day they shared with one another what they were learning and talked over plans for moving their project toward completion.

I remembered what I had always loved about teaching as I sat with them over meatloaf sandwiches, talking about projects we were currently working on, and sharing interesting facts we had uncovered. They enchanted me as only the young can, viewing life from a perspective that is nearly all future, unfazed by limits I see which, in truth, may not be limits at all for them. The possibilities are far larger than the problems. Things are going to be all right. Such are the gifts youth bring us.

LIVING IN STORIES

The work Jeff's students were doing made sense to them. They were particular people living in a particular place, and the history of that place had quite a lot to do with who they were and what their prospects were. They had become self-consciously a part of that place's history, adding their stories to its heritage. Their presentation would become a permanent part of the town's archives, saved forever in the local museum where it would be added to presentations done by students in earlier years. Some of the students even attended "school" one period a day at the museum, where they could work directly with professionals on the real work of museums: organizing the archives and preparing exhibits. This was taking museum education much further than the usual tour or other preformulated experiences organized from small twists of other people's understandings.

The story of school, or at least of this one class, had a real place in the personal story of their lives. They were engaged.

"Narrative" and "story" have become popular words, used so often and in so many ways that their meaning has become slippery. There are good reasons story has gotten so much attention in recent years. In the jostling together of various peoples and theories that characterize the modern and postmodern age, it has become increasingly clear that for humans reality has a narrative structure.

Narrative is a way of talking about events that are causally related in time, as opposed to other ways of talking about things. We can make a diagram of a toaster to see how all its parts work together, ignoring time to study the way parts are connected. When historians analyze data, such as the number of people of different races incarcerated in a particular state during a given year, they are using quantitative analysis rather than narrative to find out how things really were.

All stories are narratives but not all narratives are stories. We've all had the experience of listening to someone who narrates endlessly without quite getting to story. The talk goes on and on without a point—and then this happened, and then I said this, and then he said that, and then this happened. We want to interrupt and ask, "What's your point?"

Stories have points, which is to say they have endings. They have form—some structure that leads to the end, that moment when meaning clicks home like the punch line of a joke. To transform narrative into story, we find the form, and to see the form we must grasp the meaning.

Humans naturally encode and decode meaning in stories. Philosopher Alasdair MacIntyre (1981) tells us that "It is through hearing stories about wicked stepmothers, lost children, good but misguided kings, wolves that suckle twin boys, youngest sons who receive no inheritance but must make their own way in the world and eldest sons who waste their inheritance on riotous living and go into exile to live with the swine, that children learn or mislearn both what a child is and what a parent is, what the cast of characters may be in the drama into which they are born and what the ways of the world are. Deprive children of stories and you leave them unscripted, anxious stutterers in their actions as in their words."

We form our identity and our character through dialogic processes with our narrative environment. In practice, our identity is inseparable from our life story, and it is during adolescence that we come to understand our life as a story. Teenagers are developing an autobiographical perspective on life, understanding in ways younger children do not that their beliefs and their character traits are formed by the experiences they have had. They are learning the ways we "author" the moral stances that define us by the way we respond to the narrative flow of experience. Younger kids imagine themselves as heroes in fantasies quite unrelated to the facts of their actual existence, but teens see how particular parents and particular events have given them a particular slant on life.

As young people proceed through adolescence, stories become increasingly internalized, forming the basis of their own sense of who they are. According to psychologist Dan McAdams (1993), the work of being an adolescent is often the work of digesting and interpreting experiences and putting together out of diverse influences a life story that's more or less coherent. Teenagers, he says, are in the process of becoming a story they tell themselves about who they are.

This is one of the reasons that the narrative environment that surrounds teenagers is of profound importance. In recent decades we have awakened to the ways that neglecting the narrative environment of schools—the daily narration in hallways and in teachers' lounges as well as the great formal narratives of literature and history—turns out to be as educationally unsound as we now know that ignoring the microbial environment is medically unsound. Doctors once went from patient to patient, blood and other body fluids on their hands, without washing. Patients were put into beds where sick people had just died without anyone changing the linen. Everyone was paying attention to other things.

And while we've paid attention to other things, such as the design of curricula and assessment plans and the incorporation of new technology into classrooms, we haven't talked nearly enough about the stories that, loose in our schools and communities, infect us. An increasingly toxic narrative environment is the most serious environmental crisis we face, and the one out of which other environmental crises ultimately grow.

And the narrative environment includes more than the stories that we encounter. It also includes the audiences and the opportunities to tell the stories we have made. It is in the telling that young people integrate facts, values, and differing perspectives into coherent wholes. It is by developing the capacity to tell that they grow from the diffuse and un-settled identity of late childhood into the integrated and coherent iden-tity of successful young adulthood. A good part of educating young people is providing them with audiences that hear and respond in thoughtful and humane ways.

EDUCATION AND STORIES

One powerful way to develop and improve the narrative environment of our youth is to engage them in researching and telling stories drawn from the histories of their communities and families—to work with them in completing heritage projects. Even humble and simple stories have a kind of power that's easy to overlook. Here's Bud Cheff Sr. (1994), a seventy-eight-year-old rancher from the Mission Valley in western Montana, chatting about his early life:

> Whenever Adelle and I went somewhere, or when we were returning home, I always put the money I had left into a big jar I kept buried. When I got a chance to buy the land where the ranch now sits, I dug out my money cache, and got out the jug that I had buried. I poured it all out on a tarp and counted it; I had just enough money to pay cash for that piece of land, 160 acres. There were pennies, nickels, dimes, quarters, half dol-lars, dollar bills, five, ten and twenty dollar bills.
> "I went into the house and had Adelle and all the kids come out to my shed to see what I had on my tarp, and they all just stared at it. Adelle knew I'd been saving money, but had no idea it amounted to that much and the kids were so excited because they had never seen that much money at one time. I let them each take a handful of small change and then I gathered it up, went to the courthouse in Polson, and paid for my land.

What's interesting about this little story about what Bud wants, how he sets about getting it, and what consequences follow, is how effort-lessly it encodes a host of values. Children who grow up immersed in such everyday narratives probably do not notice that Bud is teaching his understanding of the little secrets of being human: what the rules of life are, what roles are available, and how to get what is wanted. In a way that's so natural it's easy to miss, Bud teaches perseverance, postponement of gratification, affection for spouse and children, and delight in the chance to struggle for a dream. I can testify from personal experience that a person who listens to this man tell his ordinary stories about raising a family and building a ranch will feel tugs of desire to laugh more, work harder, have more friends.

Early in the twentieth century, William Graham Sumner (1906) pointed out that through everyday stories a person learns "what conduct is approved or disapproved; what kind of man is admired most; how he ought to behave in all kinds of cases; and what he ought to believe and respect." He reminds us that "all this constitutes . . . the most essential and important education."

Schools—like persons, families, and communities—are networks of stories, including the everyday stories teachers tell in the process of taking attendance and getting classes started, handling routine classroom discipline, approving or disapproving student requests, intervening in conflicts, and so on. To get a grasp on what a school actually teaches, as opposed to what it merely espouses, visit the teachers' lounge or hang out in the hallways and listen to the stories about students, parents, and administrators. This will give you a reasonable guide to a school's moral intelligence.

It's a truism that we will educate mostly through stories whether intentionally or not. Even if we decided to avoid stories and to stick to analyses and explanations and the conveyance of facts stripped of narrative context—well, that decision and its consequences would become our story.

CHAPTER 2

Learning as Story

Reality is a story—not just a tale that is told but a story that is really so.

—Robert P. Roth

Ask someone to tell you the most important thing he or she has learned, and you will be told a story. Deep learning always takes the form of a story. The most important stories in education often aren't the ones we are told but the ones we live. To be deeply changed requires a quest with our emotions and desires engaged, so a powerful education is necessarily an adventure that can be narrated. Our desires drive us toward action. We see what we need to do. When we act—and, as John Dewey (1916) knew, thinking is sometimes our most important form of action—we encounter obstacles which require further action. It is in trying to reach goals despite obstacles, attempting work, that we experience growth and change—that is, learning. Desire and action—these are the basics not just of stories but of all learning.

DEEP LEARNING

The obvious way to get the power of narrative into schooling is to attempt real work. Jeff Gruber's class had taken the form of a story. It had become an expedition—a journey into the history of the community. He engaged students' desires by inviting them to ask real questions. What does our future hold? Why have things turned out as they have? Who has the power to affect our lives here? What can we say to them?

The students themselves suggested what action followed from their desire—let's tell our story to the corporate leaders whose decisions affect this place. Encouraged and cajoled into asking real questions and guided in the pursuit of good answers, students saw how learning leads us to view the world differently. They became protagonists in their own story: meeting opportunities, making decisions, and arriving at conclusions.

The process that Jeff used with his students was designed to promote deep learning by turning classroom work into a story in which students/protagonists identified concerns, asked questions, pursued knowledge, and formed conclusions. They understood that in doing their research they were creating a valuable legacy to add to the community's record of itself. When learning becomes a project that aims at creating a new cultural artifact, it also becomes a story.

A learning expedition is an in-depth exploration of a topic. Usually, expedition team members all research the same general question, though their individual research questions vary. The goal is to find what is in the library and then to go beyond that, bringing back new knowledge through the use of interviews, readings in primary documents, field observations at events or specific sites, or experiments.

A good learning expedition has several important characteristics:

- It has a mission: to bring back new knowledge (starting with a question and a survey of existing knowledge).
- It requires teamwork. An expedition is both the mission and the group who undertakes that mission (teams feature both cooperation and individual accountability).
- It becomes a story (expedition members are protagonists in their own quest).
- It ends in a gift of scholarship (research is service; scholarship is a gift to the community).

To guide expeditions in the Montana Heritage Project we taught teachers the ALERT process, which I developed after extensive study of comprehensive learning models. I identified the processes most such models shared, then arranged these processes into an acronym that's easy for students to remember: Ask, Listen, Explore, Reflect, Teach. In practice, the five processes overlap and flow into one another and may occur in any order. Deep learning is a recursive process, in which some tasks are interrupted by other tasks, and tasks that were set aside earlier are returned to, and new insights lead to revisions, and gaps are worked around until a way of bridging them is found. With such caveats in mind, the ALERT process can help with planning and monitoring the work, both at the beginning and along the way. When we are in the middle of things and feel confused, pausing to review the processes can help us see a useful next step. The important thing is to recognize that all the processes are involved in deep learning and that therefore they should all be structured into learning projects.

I've used this process with teachers and students at all grade levels. It works in fifth-grade classrooms, but it is also the basic pattern of doctoral dissertations. Most doctoral students begin the dissertation process by posing a hypothesis or forming a research question (*asking* a question), then move on to reviewing the literature (*listening* to the historical record), formulating and implementing a research methodology (*exploring* beyond the published record), interpreting and evaluating what happened in the light of enduring questions (*reflecting* on possible meanings), and preparing a report or presentation based on findings (*teaching* what was learned).

THE ALERT PROCESS

It might be helpful to see how the processes work by examining them in a real life expedition: the Lewis and Clark expedition, known as the Corps of Discovery.

Ask: The story of the Corps of Discovery began with a rigorous formulation of questions. The big question, of course, was what was out there? Thomas Jefferson quickly focused this to what "useful knowledge" might be found. Jefferson spent months conferring with Meriwether Lewis, and many others, discussing which questions should be asked and how they might be answered. In the instructions that came from this process, Jefferson listed dozens of specific questions about flora, fauna, rivers, soils, climates, and peoples. What could the land be used for? What possibilities for trade existed? What agricultural or commercial opportunities might be developed?

Until we have a question, it's hard to learn anything. The name we give information we aren't looking for or don't need is "noise." Every teacher has had the experience of having their finely wrought utterings screened out as so much elevator music. In John Dewey's term, learning begins with a "felt difficulty."

For students, schooling stretches out before them into seeming infinity. The great project of human knowledge has been going on for a long while and a tremendous amount of information has been gathered, constructed, organized, and published. In conventional schooling, the student's task is to take in all this preformulated knowledge.

But not many of us are interested in information for information's sake. This is not a failing but a necessity for survival. No one can pay attention to everything, but everyone has to pay attention to some things. Even before the information revolution, the amount of information available to any person at any place at any moment was potentially infinite. Sitting in an ordinary room, a person could count the holes in the ceiling tile, figure out the temperature gradients from the floor to the ceiling, analyze the furniture spacing according to Chinese philosophy, ascertain the thickness of the window glass, calculate the board feet of lumber used to manufacture the baseboards, assess likely emotional responses to various fabric colors, estimate the foot candles of light from the fluorescent fixtures, and calculate the watts used in an average year. But most people don't busy themselves with such things. A person whose interests are too promiscuous, who constantly pursues information for its own sake rather than for purposes, is odd.

Lewis and Clark had a focus that helped them sort through infinite details looking for what was pertinent and useful. They were not looking for a city of gold; they were not looking for a Fountain of Youth; they were not looking for sites for Christian missions; and they were not looking for wives and homesteads.

The process of coming to questions is central to learning, whether for students or professionals. The choice of questions guides the entire process, and reforming questions along the way is a vital part of incorporating new information into the process. The habit of converting problems, dilemmas, and opportunities into questions answerable through research is a fundamental scholarly habit.

And, in what is not at all a coincidence, it turns out that the most powerful motivation for students is not an extrinsic reward (or threat), such as a grade or a movie on Friday, but a compelling question. The main work of a human organism is to organize meaning. It's what we were meant to do. Once we have a question that moves us, we are well on our way to becoming explorers and detectives.

Listen/Look: Listening and looking refers to research into the existing historical record. Once we have a basic question, we refine it by finding out what is already known. Before the Lewis and Clark expedition got underway, its planners, led by Thomas Jefferson, labored for months listening to what was known to develop the right questions. Jefferson read many texts and sought advice from dozens of people with scientific interests. He sought news from everyone who had been up either the Mississippi or the Columbia River to increase his chances of guessing accurately what might lay between them.

Lewis began by asking what equipment and supplies would be needed then discussed possible scenarios with many experts and listened to their advice and suggestions. How many men? With what knowledge and skills? What supplies for food, medicine, clothing, and trade? What provisions for defense? What scientific instruments? The explorers scrutinized what was already known as well as what processes others had developed for exploring, experimenting, and observing to gather new knowledge.

At key points in the learning process, it is important to review the existing knowledge and examine work that has already been completed. This is the library phase of research. It is critical not only because it helps focus questions, it also provides the learner with a repertoire of research strategies and it familiarizes the learner with others who share similar concerns—kindred spirits, so to speak—who may be the best resources in the future.

Explore: The explorations are the best-known part of the Lewis and Clark expedition, and they will also be the most memorable and exciting parts of most student heritage projects. In the exploration phase of learning, we extend knowledge beyond what already exists in the historical record.

Expedition members conducted extensive interviews with Native Americans along the way; they made detailed notes and sketches of fish, wildlife, and plants they encountered; they took painstaking celestial readings to calculate precise locations; and they made critical decisions on the basis of all that was known. Dozens of plants and animals were first identified by these explorers. They noted such details as the way the Nez Perce gelded horses, and they described games played by the Chinooks.

One dramatic example of the way that our explorations lead us to confront the unexpected occurred on June 2, 1805. The Corps of Discovery arrived at a fork in the river that no one had warned them would be there. This presented a serious dilemma. Since they were seeking the best water route to traverse the continent, they had to follow the Missouri to get as near as possible to the Columbia, which they knew lay on the other side of the mountains.

They had neither time nor energy for a mistake. Meriwether Lewis noted in his journal that "to ascend [the wrong] stream . . . would not only lose us the whole of this season, but would probably so dishearten the party that it might defeat the expedition altogether."

So they looked things over carefully. The northern fork of the river was muddy, just as the Missouri had been throughout their journey. Most of the men thought this was the correct fork to follow. But the captains thought the river should be getting clearer if it was coming out of the mountains. They thought the southern fork was the right one.

They could have voted. They could have flipped a coin. But since they were scholars of a sort, they used what they already knew, in this case, about river hydrology and geography, and they combined this with hard homework. One team spent days following the muddy northern fork—which they named the Marias—a meandering forty miles. As the river wound out into the endless Canadian prairie, the captains decided to bet their expedition on the theory that the other fork would be the shortest route to the Columbia.

They were right. The expedition was made up of such challenges daily and weekly. New information had to be reconciled with existing knowledge, leading to new theories to test and new learning strategies to attempt.

For students today, research can involve exploration of historic sites, exploration of various points of view represented by living community members, and exploration of various academic disciplines and their methodologies for converting ignorance to knowledge. A spirit of adventure grows quite naturally when we begin responding to new questions, confusions, and opportunities that present themselves as we push forward.

Reflect: Reflection is analogous to the physical process of digestion: it is the way we convert facts into meanings, so we can use them. When we interpret and evaluate our experience, we are reflecting on it. Lewis and Clark did this through private pondering, as we all do, but they also did it through discussions and journal writing.

The most powerful reflection is triggered by contemplation of large and important questions—essential questions, if you will. Though essential questions are sometimes too big and unanswerable to research directly, they should be posed at the beginning of an expedition and they should be returned to regularly. Jeff's students were researching economics and the environment decade by decade through Libby's history. A typical research question might be how did people survive when the mills shut down during the Great Depression? It's an answerable question. Some of the essential questions that they contemplated were "How are people shaped by adversity?" and "How does our relationship to the land change through time?" These aren't questions that can be finally answered, but they can be reflected upon as the research progresses.

Writing is usually an important part of the reflection process. Since the Lewis and Clark expedition was planned as a learning project from the outset, they worked hard at figuring things out and writing them down. It is one of the best documented of all early exploratory projects. Donald Jackson (2000) notes that they were the "writingest explorers of their time. They wrote constantly and abundantly, afloat or ashore, legibly and illegibly, and always with an urgent sense of purpose."

This was not an accident. Thomas Jefferson insisted that detailed journals be kept by several people. Both Lewis and Clark kept journals and they ordered their sergeants "to keep a separate journal from day to day of all passing occurrences, and such other observations on the country &c. as shall appear to them worthy of notice."

Experiences we do not reflect upon tend to disappear from short-term memory before we learn what they have to teach. As events and information tend to press in on us, the past is continually being swallowed by the present, and it is easy, in school or in life, to continue moving on to new things without pausing to consider what it all means. "An unexamined life," Socrates observed, "is not worth living." Through reflection, new knowledge is incorporated into existing knowledge, information is manipulated and tested, new questions are posed and new avenues for exploration are considered. Of all the stages of learning, reflection is the one that is most often neglected, though it is the one where most learning occurs.

Quite likely, the fondest academic memories you have are of discussion sessions, where you and other students and, if you were lucky, a teacher or two, sat around and played with what you were studying. Nothing is more fun than thinking.

Teach/Tell: The best strategy for learning something is to teach it. Students in school should be doing much more teaching. We can teach by giving presentations, writing articles, creating graphics, or doing multimedia presentations. It is in using our research to create gifts of scholarship that we really engage the material at a level that makes it ours.

After the expedition was over, Clark converted his extensive navigational notes into finished maps (that are amazingly accurate). When Lewis reported in person to Jefferson, Jefferson noted that he spread the maps out on the floor and "examined these sheets myself minutely." What a gift of scholarship!

One of the greatest disappointments of the expedition is that Meriwether Lewis had tremendous difficulty with the Teach/Tell stage. He never even began writing his final report though it had been promised to publishers and was eagerly awaited by Jefferson. His failure to put his thoughts and experiences into final form was a loss both for him personally and for the nation. His suicide not long after the expedition is likely related to this failure. People who commit suicide often suffer from a kind of narrative dysfunction: they can no longer make satisfactory meaning of the story of their lives.

To learn is to change: to transform ourselves and our world. It is in making something new that we refine our critical abilities, move from vague and confusing impressions to precise formulations and make our own contributions to the ongoing project of improving our knowledge.

Heritage projects can culminate in public exhibitions and performances that give researchers a chance to show what they've learned at the same time the new work is given back to the community in a form that will be useful for later learners. Both students and adults find hard work more gratifying when they understand they are creating a legacy for others in the form of new cultural artifacts.

Final products might include a transcript of discussions or interviews, a radio show, a magazine or pamphlet, a website, a dramatic production, a research report, a public forum, a museum display, a video, a collection of indexed oral history audio tapes, a photo essay, or any number of other products. Though the processes are crucial, the best way to ensure high-quality processes is to strive for high-quality products.

Creating gifts of scholarship has everything to do with standards and accountability. When student heritage projects aim at the creation of final products of lasting worth for an audience beyond the teacher, standards flow from the demands of actual situations—such as the need for accuracy and elegance in a museum display—rather than arbitrary-appearing teacher rules. The connections between classroom work and the real world are developed and clarified, and standards move from being bureaucratic noise to being the secret of success.

When the public presentation of academic work becomes part of a school's and a community's culture, the standards are not set by a minimum that some testing service will accept, but they are set by the best performances. At a statewide Youth Heritage Festival sponsored by the Montana Heritage Project, students from around the state present the research they did during the year. The performances get better each year. After all, students are performing for their peers, and though some performances are weaker than others, these are mostly ignored. Students watch and learn from the best that they see, because when they stand up in front of a large audience to show what they have done, they want to be a hit. Teachers leading such projects are as accountable as basketball coaches: they can't hide.

These ALERT processes form the basis for a school culture that promotes high expectations, quality work, and strong efforts toward learning—they encourage young people to make learning and contributing to the community an important part of the story of their own lives.

Heritage projects are not just for kids. They are also the basis for building a culture of scholarship in the community outside the classroom window. By exploring near at hand questions in the company of others, any of us can share the spirit of the Corps of Discovery. We engage. We wake up. We become more alert. We live more deeply, more precisely attuned to the world around.

When groups set out on their own quests for understanding, they soon become protagonists in a fresh story, finding themselves explorers in unmapped terrain. As we work to use our learning to transform at least some little part of our world, we move toward understanding, and we develop the robust self-confidence we can never have except through genuine accomplishment. In some ways our task seems harder than it did for those courageous explorers, who, after all, had before them in vivid form an unknown continent. Today, it's easy to be discouraged because it seems that the world has all been mapped and little real work is left for would-be explorers. All that's left for us is a series of worksheets stretching to infinity. This view is reinforced by many textbooks, which are written in the voice of disembodied authority, as though everything is known or things had to turn out as they did.

But as the Libby students learned, the local past is a vast and largely unexplored domain. It is as strange and exotic as anything Lewis and Clark encountered. Any of us in our neighborhoods and towns can partake of the zest and adventure that Lewis and Clark knew.

CHAPTER 3

Stories and Place Making

> The rudiments of moral action—a regard for the well-being of others and anxiety at having failed to perform to a standard—are present well before anything like moral reasoning could occur.
>
> —James Q. Wilson

THE HEROIC URGE

In 1849 Kit Carson set off in pursuit of a band of Jicarilla Apaches who had captured a white woman (White, 1991). The anecdote, related by Carson himself, sounds like the beginning of a movie. However, Carson had to ride his sweating horse not through the West of some scriptwriter's imagination, but through a world more like the one we experience every day. A world where we lose the trail, move too slowly, lose our nerve, take the wrong turn, arrive too late or in the wrong place. By the time Carson caught up with the Apaches, the woman was dead.

In the abandoned Apache camp he found something else though—a book about a largely fictional character named "Kit Carson" who was a great Indian-slaying hero. It was a shock to him. According to historian Richard White, "Carson's reaction to finding the book . . . was to lament his failure to live up to his fictional reputation." The actual Kit Carson was something less than godlike. He couldn't tuck his pants into a pair of colorful boots, swoop into the scene amid a glittering whirl of rhinestones and leather fringe to perform six-gun magic against the hidden forces of evil. Compared to pulp fiction, real life seemed a bit drab. And so "the fictional Carson became the standard for the real Carson." His life began imitating the story.

It's always been this way. There are stories and images loose in the world that capture us, filling us with visions of how we want to be. Such stories rival geography and economics as forces that shape the history both of individuals and of nations. When Shelley said that "poets are the unacknowledged legislators of the world," what he meant was that folks make the world they live in out of the worlds they imagine. Imaginative descriptions of reality—that is, poetry, in its broadest sense—are the stuff of place making, which is the basis of world making.

Like Kit Carson, each of us is looking for a storyline that frees us to be the heroes we know we were meant to be. And in truth, the plot of every life is that of a heroic quest. Life asks everything of us, sooner or later. All of us have faced Goliath, all of us have been given impossible labors, all of us have had to take decisive action without knowing what we will unleash, and all of us have faced moments where it was up to us to put the times aright. Not to see this is to fail.

If we do not provide our youth with a hero's education, then we may not be educating them so much as corrupting them. The essence of corruption, after all, is to retreat from the heroic call and to distract ourselves with lesser things.

I have spent many hours talking with good teachers, and something they have in common is that each of them in his or her special way lives heroically, pushing against limits and enlarging the world's possibilities through a quiet kind of generosity and courage that arises, I think, from faith in freedom. Time is opportunity and the past only rough-hews the future; it does not determine it. What we do matters.

Few things are sadder than a school where the teachers have given up and are just getting through the day, counting the minutes till the bell or the years till the pension. The school where I became principal was a low-performance place. Few demands were put on either teachers or students. They bellyached, as people in such places normally do, and it took me a while to understand that the complaining did not signify desire for change. Things were easy, and the teachers who had stayed didn't really want things to be hard, in the way things worth doing so often are.

I changed the schedule to allow longer periods and restructured the teachers' workday to allow teamwork and reorganized the curriculum to promote deeper engagement in a few important topics. As these changes went into effect and I watched how people reacted, I saw that such structural changes were superficial.

The main issue in school reform will always be people and what they believe and what they desire. What a teacher believes and desires, and how he or she enacts that belief and desire, will have ten times the effect of any other factor in determining whether students move forward or regress. "Everything in education," according to presidential adviser Philip Howard (2001), "comes down to people on the spot." And yet teachers feel constrained against drawing on their passion, personality, or judgment within a system where compliance matters more than intelligence, industry, or responsibility.

Official education today is a din of competing narratives, and teachers and principals, who try to keep up with organizational standards, procedures, requirements, and reforms emanating from all directions, often become exhausted, even as pressure groups lobby for more, trying to get control of what is taught by getting control of the official language. The official language becomes an aspect of the problem—a deadening agglomeration that stifles thought and garbles communication. When we look at the dense webs of bureaucratic processes that confront any parent or teacher or student who simply wants to get to work with others on exciting scholarship rather than to be entangled in endless committee meetings that only talk about such work—or even worse fight about it—it can seem hopeless.

After thousands of studies, hundreds of policy changes, and dozens of new programs, we aren't likely to make a lot of difference by tinkering with variables such as budget allocations and class size, though both money and smaller classes make things easier. And we aren't going to make significant headway by tinkering with flow charts to change the structure or timing of events as they unfold, though confused systems certainly don't help. And we aren't going to find a new workshop model that will build consensus among people whose interests are in conflict, though talking, if it is honest, is not a bad idea.

The root of our problems with school is that members of our communities inhabit different stories and so we cannot stop arguing. Debates between people who inhabit different stories seldom work. People can even agree about facts and still disagree about causes, meanings, and best responses. Was it Descartes who described the trouble people have when they do not grant anyone enough authority to make decisions? They are like a group of people lost in the woods, arguing about which way is the best way out. Though any direction taken and held to would lead out of the woods, people can't agree so instead of going anywhere they continue arguing and remain lost. There are lots of good ways to operate a school, but politically governed bureaucracies among people who do not share a common moral vision tend to implement none of them. Though discussion about differences is necessary and frequently useful, mere contention is always a waste of time if not worse.

Getting people to join a different story is a different thing. It's not mostly a matter of persuading them they are wrong. It's setting off on an adventure, following leads, tracking down clues, and imagining other worlds. It's a matter of possibilities—a new world.

The truth is that people are looking for stories to join. We are social animals, forming groups at every turn. Our language teems with names for different kinds of groups formed for different purposes: gangs, crews, factions, squads, mobs, teams, cliques, tribes, orders, juntas, guilds, neighborhoods, parties, and troupes. We band together naturally and instinctively, and it is usually an organizing story that brings us to community. Plato's Academy, Hitler's Third Reich, the Army of Northern Virginia, Rockefeller's Standard Oil, the Sierra Club, and the Montana Vigilantes can each be understood as the enactment of a particular story.

COMMUNITIES AS SHARED NARRATIVES

When hunters gather around a campfire to hear stories, maybe about a wounded buck tracked for miles before the killing was finished, the individual is sharing, preserving his notions of proper conduct and effective technique. Such stories form the communal memories and the communal mores. "A good hunter doesn't leave a wounded animal in the woods. We are good hunters."

Middle-class folks today make the characteristic middle-class organization—the bureaucracy—work in large part by swapping tales at the water cooler about how to use the grievance procedure, the meaning of office changes, unofficial communications routes, and the like. The organization's character is a piece of those stories. Some bureaucracies are crisp, efficient, and competent. Some are distrustful, confused, and murky. When organizations are changing, divergent and sometimes incompatible stories circulate. Few people enjoy this. An unsettled narrative environment leaves people unsure of themselves and their roles.

Our consciousness is formed of the stories into which, throughout our lives, we continue awakening. Coming to consciousness is a process of internalizing social structures: what begins as the society around us becomes the structure of our minds. The Russian psychologist Lev Vygotsky (1988) points out that when children who can speak begin playing, adopting roles such as "mother" or "sister," they are escaping the world that is immediately before them and acting in a world of cognition. They can even interact with nonexistent objects, feeding an imaginary baby with an imaginary bottle. But those nonexistent objects, the very stuff of mental life, originated in the world outside the mind.

In the fossilized metaphors that make up ordinary conversation we can glimpse how deeply our thinking is shaped by stories that operate on us all but unconsciously. The linguist George Lakoff (1980) points out that we are taught that an argument is a war. He shows the way this organizing metaphor can be glimpsed in statements such as these: "Your claims are indefensible. He attacked every weak point in my argument. His criticisms were right on target. I demolished his arguments. He shot down all my arguments."

It's conceivable that we might think of an argument as a dance, but we don't. Sometimes, though, we do think of arguments as journeys. Lakoff points out that when we are thinking this way, we say such things as: "We have set out to prove that bats are birds. When we get to the next point, we shall see that philosophy is dead. So far, we've seen that no current theories will work. Our goal is to show that hummingbirds are essential to military defense."

Maybe the most powerful work of education is accomplished by embedding young people in shared narratives that organize what they see and hear, that set limits, explain events, encode strategies, give form to aspirations, and preserve memories—all while weaving moments, weeks, and years into patterns of meaning—that is, providing them an educative narrative environment by surrounding them with communities that live what needs to be taught. Parents and citizens and teachers who want to reform schools would do well to realize that they contend not against people but against metaphors and stories. If they are too soon distracted into chatter about tests, standards, budgets, schedules—the five-year plans and new deals of contemporary schooling—they are unlikely to make much headway. It's worth noticing how little of what is published in education journals or talked about in education classrooms has to do with teaching and learning. The bulk of it has to do with how to interact with the systems we have built—strategies for communicating in large bureaucracies, tactics for implementing new schedules, and processes for staying in touch with various stakeholders.

We need such thinking, to be sure, but we need to pinch ourselves from time to time to wake up and remember that none of it is teaching or learning. Mistaking means for ends is the great seduction of big organizations. Those with power and authority spend the hours of their lives swamped with details related to the means, and it's hard not to begin thinking such is the real work. But it isn't.

Good teachers are doing the real work. Researchers routinely study the Internet connectivity in classrooms, the dollars in budgets, the electives in the curriculum, the economic status of students and teachers, the minutes spent in various activities, and hundreds of other aspects of school, but hardly ever the narrative environment within which students and teachers make sense of their lives.

Sometimes just returning to teaching and learning reveals that we don't need to solve long-standing problems. Sometimes, when we embark on a new story, old troubles dematerialize.

Nikki was one of my students who used to drop by after class to talk. She was only a high school sophomore, and much of her conversation focused on her drinking and her tangled love life. She had bright red hair and all the problems that preoccupy so many young people today: not just drugs but also an unwise and undisciplined sex life and a poor academic record. I disapproved of all that, which I think is why Nikki talked to me about it. She disapproved too but was caught in a mess she didn't yet know how to handle.

In class we were reading *The Chosen,* a novel by Chaim Potok I had selected because its central theme is the romance of scholarship and because it offered a way to introduce Jewish culture to kids who knew no Jewish folks. The protagonist, Danny, is engaged in a heroic quest to study and to understand. His dream and his drive is to be a scholar.

One afternoon Nikki leaned her chin in her hands and said, "I want to be like Danny."

Having her say that so directly and simply caught me by surprise, even though some such outcome was surely my goal in choosing the book. On the surface her life had little in common with Danny's. But I knew from my own life story that real education often isn't happening on the surface, where usual educational measurements focus. To really change our lives, first we need to see that other lives are possible and then we need to desire them. At the moment, Nikki couldn't get free of her bad habits, but reading had planted in her the seeds from which freedom grows: a better story, a different desire. Kids who are surrounded by badness need many things, not the least of which are visions of ways life might be that are found in history, literature, and art. Nothing is more useful than a good story. The last time I talked with Nikki was when she contacted me for a recommendation to law school. She was on the dean's list.

Unfortunately, it's not just good stories that have power. The Romans of the late empire staged raw and brutal stories in real life in their arenas: the planet was ransacked for beasts to tear apart convicts and slaves for afternoon entertainment. They came to crave ever bloodier spectacles—gladiators striving to survive amid the oozing and splattering of blood, gorgeously red under the merciless Mediterranean sun. They transformed themselves into a people who took their greatest pleasure in watching pain and bloodshed. Children, educated by the stories they knew, amused themselves by torturing animals.

Though for us such entertainments are most often "only" simulated by movie companies rather than happening in actuality, to the human imagination such a distinction sometimes matters little. People living in real life stories that are full of gentle and loving companionship may be able to watch violent movies without developing a taste for real-life gore, but none of us can isolate our lives from the lives of others for whom movies constitute social reality. As the Vandals began destroying

Carthage, Sumner (1906) observed, people were slow to react because they thought the cries of people slaughtered in the streets came from the arena. The death throes of that civilization became indistinguishable from its entertainments.

In America today, after years of gradually coarsening music and movie fare, one needn't always buy a ticket to hear the fire of automatic weapons or the screams of victims. As the marketers of tobacco did for decades, today's merchants of vicarious vice dispute a causal connection between their movies and the real-world effects. To deny that violent entertainments contribute to violent lives is to deny the power of imagination and art. We do what we repeatedly think, and, as Aristotle pointed out, we are what we repeatedly do.

THE SOCRATIC WAY OF NOT KNOWING

Seeing that we are educated by stories and communities awakens us to a set of new problems. In Greece before Socrates, the great poets—storytellers such as Homer—were widely understood to be the primary educators of youth. Learning the stories *was* getting an education. But Socrates knew lots of people who had been educated in that way, and he found them lacking. In a nutshell, he saw that people educated by stories remained governed by passion. He thought they would be better off governed by reason—by philosophy.

His method can be seen most clearly in the stories told about him by his student, Plato. One day Socrates was hanging out, which he did a lot. Euthyphro came by in something of a hurry. Euthyphro's father had mistreated a servant, and Euthyphro knew that was wrong. Socrates was intrigued by Euthyphro's intention to drag his own father into court over the affair. So he began asking questions, beginning with the obvious: why?

"Piety" compelled him to it, said Euthyphro, naively thinking that would clarify the matter.

Socrates, of course, was a deep thinker, so for him things were not so simple. Socrates wanted to know what piety was. Since Euthyphro was so certain about his piety, maybe he could help by explaining things. People who are sure they know what's right are often eager to help others know it too, so Euthyphro tried to answer Socrates' inquiries by telling some stories that illustrate piety.

This is normal. If someone asks to know what "red" is, it's easier to point to several red things than it is to define "redness." We know in a practical way many things we can't define. If someone asks what "courage" might be, we are usually content to point to courageous actions by telling stories.

Unfortunately for Euthyphro, that isn't the kind of understanding Socrates was after. Stories? He wanted definitions. He wanted lines drawn around things so he could know exactly what they are and what they aren't. Precision is the Socratic goal. Without precision, how can we dissolve our confusion? So Socrates questioned everything Euthyphro told him, splitting ever finer hairs. No matter which way Euthyphro turned, Socrates followed with an even harder question. Endless, endless questioning in search of ever finer precision. Socrates wanted things clear.

But of course, they don't get clear. By the end of the dialogue, Euthyphro had completely lost his bearings, unable to answer anything to Socrates' satisfaction. He wasn't sure any more what piety might be. Socrates didn't know either but he had said all along that he was smarter than other people not because of what he knew, but because he knew he didn't "know" things, while other people supposed they knew a great deal. By the time Aristotle made his list of the virtues a couple generations later, "piety" had disappeared. Today, most people would feel insulted to be described as "pious."

In the age of electron microscopes, we know that there are no lines around things. With sufficient magnification, every boundary disappears. The universe, after all, is one thing. Our questions can also dissolve all lines. We can question everything, becoming like graduate students who see through everything. Ironically, for the person who sees through everything, the world becomes invisible. To see through everything is to see nothing. When his fellow Athenians put Socrates to death for corrupting the youth of Athens by teaching them to question the gods, they may have had a point. He did constitute a threat to a way of life.

Socrates, to be sure, is one of our great teachers. The Socratic way of knowing is to expose ignorance, of which there is a great deal, and ignorance remains as great an enemy of peace and prosperity today as it ever did. No people has escaped the plague of false gods, the ones we make ourselves. When, with due deliberation, a democracy sentenced Socrates to death, his student, Plato, who loved both Socrates and the Athens that killed him, set about the labor of conceiving a government where reason truly would rule, where the philosopher might be safe. His powerful thoughts guided generations through experiments and reflections, and the ideal of reason gained ground—not rapidly but relentlessly. Plato banned the storytellers from his ideal republic. The passions were to be governed by reason. The king might let the poets back in, but only when they had been tamed, telling only those stories that reason deemed fit.

Plato knew that conduct was governed by emotions and that emotions were governed by stories. He also knew that stories didn't need to be true to be successful—that false gods often ruled the earth, keeping people in the chains of superstition, ignorance, and tradition. What was needed, then, was to select by reason the stories fit for children.

This was not the way the ancient world worked. Alexander the Great thought that his might and glory were reason enough to justify his cruel and barbaric conduct, and none of his contemporaries condemned him for being unreasonable. He was, they noted with awe, glorious.

And yet, millennia later, most governments appeal to reason rather than to honor or glory or kinship to justify their actions, no matter how loopy their reasoning sometimes seems to their opponents. This can be counted a success for the Socratic way of knowing. It's taken a couple millennia, but much of the world now bows in homage to the ideal of the philosopher king, to the idea that we should be ruled by laws and that the laws should derive from reason.

We can be grateful that we are not governed by the whims of monarchs but by systems of our own design. The systems of social machinery we've invented—bureaucracies—are not operated by poets and storytellers but by folks with doctorates who subordinate their passions to the research and to the rationalized process. They make decisions, or seem to, after gathering reams of evidence and exchanging dozens of memos in which multiple possibilities are subjected to analysis. Objectivity and impersonality are the hallmarks of acceptable style.

There's a kind of glory in all that. Bureaucracies run on rationales and they encourage knowing, which is difficult. Being a philosopher king is hard work.

Creating such organizations has been a triumph in many ways. Living by the rule of law can be ennobling, and modern bureaucracies instill real virtues: control of ego, diplomacy, pleasantness, patience, awareness of complexity, and skill with abstractions and concepts. Few of us would like to go back to the good-old-boy networks and kinship bands formed by blood loyalty that to a great degree our bureaucracies have replaced.

And yet, all is not well.

Though we can trust our bureaucracies to be rational, we cannot as easily trust them to be good. We saw quite clearly in the twentieth century that rationalized bureaucracies can use the tools of reason to serve the most base of passions. National Socialism grew out of the intelligentsia and such were its earliest supporters. The Nazi machinery worked through reasons, explanations, measurements, laws, and new definitions of sickness and health. If "rule of law" means simply obedience to the laws that come into being, then the Nazis had it down. The workings of the Third Reich would seem quite familiar to the inhabitant of many modern bureaucracies. The physicist Richard Feynman said that a man in a Buddhist temple once told him: "To every man is given the key to the gates of heaven. The same key opens the gates of hell." So it is with science, Feynman said. And with all reason. Even the love of reason, we now see, is, like other loves, a passion.

The trouble is that although philosophy can dethrone false gods, it cannot itself establish a true god. It has within it no basis for morality. The Socratic quest was, after all, a quest for goodness, perfectly understood. We soon see that reason doesn't necessarily lead to goodness. The Enlightenment failed to show how morality could be derived from reason although it did succeed in dethroning religion, and in the wake of its failure, the human sciences abandoned morality—normative views—which came to seem only a baseless set of value judgments—backed by the authority of neither God nor of science. The hope persisted for some time that reason itself could guide us toward some governing sense of decency, but history has not been kind to that hope.

Reason, like the language of which it is made, is a power, but also like language, it has no moral content of its own. As a god itself, reason is decidedly false.

Where does this leave young people, who are schooled in modern bureaucracies from which the poets have been mostly exiled, which will not speak persuasively about what is good? Bureaucratic schools make a particular kind of education likely. Some years ago I did a study of the literature of teaching. Not what's called the professional literature produced by researchers using models drawn from the social sciences, but stories of actual teaching told by teachers. The dominant theme running through these stories was the struggle to keep alive the heroic impulse—the passion to do something good to enlarge life's possibilities—within a machine that was indifferent to the passions of individuals.

Teachers told of a system constantly interfering with their efforts to make of their lives an ennobling and coherent story. The machine that was frustrating them was nothing other than the rationalized human organization we built to conduct our affairs according to the rule of law, which is none other than the rule of reason.

It's a trite joke that if Socrates showed up in today's schools, he would not be a likely candidate for tenure. This world, governed by reason, is still not safe for heroes, even of the philosophical variety. It was, after all, Socrates' heroism more than his philosophy that got him in trouble. And if Socrates would not be welcome in today's schools, even less would be the heroes of *The Iliad*. They obviously have more in common with the "at risk" students than with the counselors who would soon surround them with the vocabulary of adjustment. Heroes are a passionate bunch, and they have been banned.

When school people know things, they define curricula and write tests to ensure that others will know them too. They amplify their knowing, like a loudspeaker blurting administrative trivia into the classroom, silencing the din of competing worlds. The passionate quest is routinized into the daily grind, and not just students but also teachers feel silenced. We purchase canned programs then begin to feel programmed. The inertia of past solutions impede creative responses to change—that is, they impede life itself. Dead words from our past dampen conversation and dialogue. The system becomes comatose in the way everyone knows who has sat through long, late afternoon meetings where there was not the faintest hope of accomplishing anything. Knowing transforms itself into an enemy of learning.

But like a sleepy afternoon, it never lasts. Life continues. Every forest burns, eventually. After five hundred years or so, cedar groves ignite and massive trees with their dense canopy shading the under stories are reduced quite rapidly into ashes. Fire is part of the life cycle of forests. It releases back into that cycle the resources that have been locked up by earlier growth.

Like forests, human institutions need cleansing fires from time to time. Otherwise, they deaden into preoccupation with their own continuance, which is quite a different thing than accomplishing the mission that called them into existence. They become larger and more powerful as they become more disconnected from reality. Wise people give new leaders enough power to change and reorganize the institutions they lead bit by bit, lest some spark set in motion high-speed, large-scale change.

The evidence is widespread that the schools we have built are not congenial places for the best teachers, and few of the reform proposals offered by politicians deal realistically with that problem. In recent years studies claiming that small schools work better than large schools have become popular, and many huge school systems are now experimenting with ways to break themselves up into small operational units. What underlies the belief that smaller schools are better is simply a hunger for less bureaucracy and more opportunity for individual action.

Without awaiting nationwide or statewide or even district-wide restructuring, small bands of students and teachers and parents can set off on learning expeditions, neither dismantling the huge bureaucracies nor waiting for them to change but simply, to as great an extent as they can, getting on with the real work. Though the world has never been safe for heroes—it can't be—maybe we can take courage from realizing that it isn't safe for those who give up their heroic quest either.

When I talk with teachers around the country about heritage projects, they always ask how they can undertake such ambitious work, given the collapsing of the curriculum caused by the pressure of accountability defined by narrow tests. I have lots of answers that all amount to this: we do what we can in whatever circumstances we find ourselves.

I think of the Zen master who was asked by a frustrated student, "What do we do about the fact that no matter what exalted work we undertake, we are chained to necessity. Every day we have to find food and eat and every day we need to interrupt our labors to sleep. What are we to do about that?"

The master answered, "We eat. We sleep."

THE LOST PLOT

If bureaucratic schools have left behind moral clarity, it is up to communities to provide it. Schoolteachers are necessarily reluctant to speak with conviction about what is good and what is bad, except on the shrinking list of topics about which there is cultural consensus. But it is not necessary for a neighborhood's grandparents and mayors and artists to be so coy. They speak as free citizens rather than as agents of the state, and they have a lot to say that young people need to hear. They give no tests and enforce no obedience. They simply tell their stories. It's enough.

Good people are often quite simple, while bad people nearly always seem quite complex. People who are straying from what they know is right have to justify themselves and they generally do this by complicating the issues. Much of the complexity we face today is a cover.

A few hundred years after Socrates, a different teacher gave his students a rule to follow. "Love thy neighbor as thyself," he said.

It seems simple enough. But of course, not everyone thought so. There's a guy in the crowd—maybe a student of Socrates'—we're not told much about him except that he's a lawyer. He wants things more precise. When should I love my neighbor? And exactly how much? There are dozens or hundreds of more or less unanswered questions we can ask about the teacher's rule. Without more precision, how will I ever be certain where my neighbor ends and I begin?

This is the question the lawyer asks: "And who is my neighbor?"

He wants a definition. Once he gets it, he can wrangle with it forever. But the teacher knows all about that sort of thing, and he doesn't answer with a definition. That way of knowing, he knows, can slip into the sophisticated form of ignorance common among lawyers. We can glimpse it in the story told about a lawyer riding through the countryside with a friend. They pass a herd of Holsteins. "Look at the spotted cows," the friend comments. The lawyer looks. "Yes, " he says. "They appear to be. On this side, at least."

As the lawyerly disposition to dissolve everything through endless questioning moves through popular culture via television talk shows focused on high-profile criminal trials, we observe more and more people who apparently believe they are only guilty of what can be proved, by either a preponderance of the evidence or, even more unlikely, beyond reasonable doubt. They begin to confuse "truth" with "proof," trying to forget that, in their hearts, they know when they are lying, which means they know more about truth than they pretend to know. Such knowledge (which can be overcome with hard study) is the bedrock upon which radical relativism crashes.

The great theme of detective novels is the search for a way through that dark region between appearances and reality: When can we say we know, and how many ways can appearances lead us to wrong conclusions? There are always those who see that dark region as an opportunity. It's no accident that the rise of the lawyerly class criminalizes society. The fact that proof is difficult works to the advantage of criminals. We make laws to constrain bad behavior, but we can always quibble over what the words mean, turning the law away from public meanings that citizens can discuss into scholarly disputations in which any understanding is tenuous and ephemeral enough for aggressors against the public good to inch forward, dissolving whatever obstructs their own will. In such a society, criminals prosper and piety dissolves, along with respect for authority, commitment to morality, and the struggle to reach high ideals.

If we are to be the sort of teachers our children need, we need to cultivate a simplicity in our stories and in our conduct that can only be achieved by people whose primary interest is to be good. We need to surround our young people with communities that care about one another and about fundamental human truths. We need to protect them from being too influenced by the lessons that bureaucracies sometimes teach, as when they reward self-interest, attention to appearances, and avoidance of risk.

When it comes to what to believe, we often make two opposite errors. First, we believe things without evidence. From malicious gossip to false history to pseudoscience, the willingness to believe and act on ideas without evidence is the source of endless misery and countless tragic wrecks in personal and national history.

But the opposite problem is just as dangerous: refusing to believe anything not yet proved, in spite of good evidence. Proof is frequently not available even though the need to act remains. The demand for proof is often a method of blocking the very demands that our sense of goodness places upon us. Questioning things can prevent some mistakes, but it can also interfere with grasping what is plain and simple.

So the teacher who knows that loving our neighbors would be a good thing deflects the lawyer's question and instead of getting lost in wrangling tells a story. "A certain man went down from Jerusalem to Jericho and fell among thieves . . ." he begins.

When he finishes his story about a Samaritan and about several people who would not help him and about one who did, the teacher turns the question back to the lawyer. "Which of these," he asks, "do you think was the man's neighbor."

"The one who helped," the lawyer answers. He knows. If he did not want to know at least weakly he could have avoided the knowledge by the simplest act of will, but it is nonetheless encoded in the story in a way that any normal human can understand.

The surprising twist in the story is not that we should love members of our family and tribe, which is ancient wisdom that all groups understand. What was new was the universality of the definition. The Samaritans were a group generally despised by the people Jesus taught, and his refusal to teach the concept of "neighbor" in a way that you or I or the lawyer could define it precisely allows his story to carry its message with great accuracy. There is no boundary where we can stop and quarrel.

By presenting his knowledge as a story rather than as a set of logical propositions, the teacher moves the focus away from how clever his listeners might be and toward what is right conduct. His point doesn't turn on a precise definition of neighbor but upon a choice between two worlds: one where strangers are prey and one where strangers help.

Having decided that one likes a neighborly world better than a world of thugs, one can find plenty of work for philosophy to do. One may ponder, for example, the difference between accuracy and precision. The story Jesus told points to an accurate understanding of neighborliness, but he frustrates the lawyer's attempt to make it more precise. Accuracy is a different thing than precision, and they tend to have a reciprocal relationship so that as you increase one you decrease the other.

In the hurly-burly of daily life, we make our way with guides that are highly accurate though not very precise. "You get more flies with honey than with vinegar." This points to an accurate understanding of one of the principles of life. To make it more precise, we could begin forming answers to such questions as "How many more flies?" "Male or female flies?" "Does it matter whether the day is sunny or overcast?"

This is the sort of knowledge that lawyers and education researchers often pursue, and it has its place, but it isn't the only kind of knowledge, and Jesus understood that when we face our most important decisions in life, we can't merely apply logic and calculation. We choose, giving our passions their voice. What we choose is the world we want. This is what we need to help our young people to see: our choices cause different sorts of worlds to come into being. Through our conduct we are makers of worlds. Or makers of places. This town, or this school, or this classroom, for example. It's a secret all good families share.

Though we can question goodness, as Socrates did, in a quest to understand it better, it's also obvious that we can question it as criminals and their attorneys do, in order to undermine it. Goodness, after all, places burdens upon us and doesn't always give us the permission we want. The initial turn against goodness can feel wonderful, a liberation, and we can soothe our conscience by becoming philosophers, quibbling over this or that definition to create confusion about whether we have really strayed much or at all, or by becoming lawyers, arguing that the standard was poorly construed, a relic of a dark past that should be replaced by a more modern and enlightened standard. We can find ways to continue feeling okay about our essential goodness.

But a time always comes when we encounter less sophisticated goodness. Then we either realize our mistake and turn back on ourselves, or we give ourselves permission to hate the goodness and attack it, feeling that it is evil—a hurtful thing that, in restoring a standard, restores our guilt.

After the thousands of books written on moral philosophy, we are left with no real defense against badness except the desire for goodness. And yet that seems to be enough, though just barely. Though goodness has lost many battles, the tide century after century seems to be on the side of good. As they find ways to do so, most people keep choosing democracy over tyranny, negotiation over battle, truth over lies, friends over enemies, and helping over hurting. And if we can't always define goodness precisely, neither can we honestly say we don't know what it is. Furthermore, we have ample reason to think that if we know, other people do too. Some biologists see strong evidence that a moral sense, rooted in love—which they prefer to call "attachment"—is the basis of our evolutionary history. We survived by forming groups of which the mother-child attachment was the basis, and the language that empowers our most spectacular achievements developed out of a primal empathy that bound us to one another. In our deepest nature, we are loving creatures.

In his study of the role reason plays in choosing our goals, neurologist Donald Calne (2001) came to the conclusion that reason has no role. He admits that "to deny that reason has a role in setting our goals seems, at first, rather odd." After all, "a personal decision to go on a diet or take more exercise appears to be based upon reason. The same might be said for a government decision to raise taxes or sign a trade treaty." But before these decisions were other decisions. "Reason is only contributing to the *how* portion of these decisions; the more fundamental *why* element, for all of these examples, is driven by instinctive self-preservation, emotional needs, and cultural attitudes."

In *Nichomachean Ethics*, even the great reasoner Aristotle expressed impatience with knowledge when it came to virtue. The issue, he says, is not to "not to know what it is, but to know whence it comes (or how to acquire it), that is what is most precious. For we do not want to know what courage is, but to be courageous, nor what justice is, but to be just, in the same way that we want to be in good health rather than to know what kind of thing health is." His profound experience of life led him to go so far as to insist that "as condition for the possession of virtues, knowledge has little or no weight at all."

Yesterday, we grew up, most of us, with access to gentling stories and ennobling tales, and whatever sorrows we've come to know, we are never farther than memory from that mythic space in which as children we began to sense what's at stake. It's a landscape of hope and transcendence—where the ugly frog is only the way a miracle looks before it happens, where the cowardly lion will find courage and where the evil tower will finally fall down. It's a kingdom where we sense more than know that just when corruption seems invincible, it meets its end quickly. It's a homeland peopled by strangers who happen along from time to time and save us, where we sense that a mighty play is unfolding, that everyone is watching and that our destiny is to be the hero. Everything is riding on us, and we only need to be good.

Most kids today are still familiar with such stories. But their narrative environment includes much more cynicism and sarcasm. They have grown up in a debunking age, surrounded by smart characters so practiced at seeing through hypocrisy that they habitually look for the dark side of any goodness, any altruism. Some of these young people need, in somewhat the way a drowning person needs a life preserver, helpful strangers and good neighbors. They need to hear the stories we know that are better than the stories we are telling.

Every good community has the storytellers it needs.

The Great, Unfinished Project

Quests sometimes fail, are abandoned or dissipated into distractions; and human lives may in all these ways also fail. But the only criteria for success or failure in a human life as a whole are the criteria of success or failure in a narrated or to-be-narrated quest.

—Alasdair MacIntyre

THE LOST LIBRARY

The story of education is itself one of the great stories. It's a story of collaboration and of gifts. It's a story of community.

Millennia ago, a great library was built in Egypt at the intersection of three continents. Though the library was destroyed centuries ago, it was the chief glory of the ancient world, and it has not been forgotten.

It will never be forgotten because it is one of the defining stories of our race. The story of any great library is more than a story about a collection: it is primarily a story about a community. What was most important about the lost Library of Alexandria was the community of scientists, artists, and writers that formed around the pursuit of knowledge. The gathering together of seven-hundred-thousand books in a single collection in a world where books were hand copied and rare was not a simple event. Rather, it was a project that brought thousands of people into collaboration over centuries to create a heritage for all peoples. Every good library lives through its community of scholars.

Alexandria itself became one of the principal cities of the world, a vast metropolis of marble. The streets were filled with people from all over the world: Macedonian soldiers, Africans, Babylonians, Syrians, Persians, Italians, and Gauls. And the library was a community made up of people of all ethnic and religious groups, drawn together in a great conversation about great subjects aimed at removing error and adding detail to our knowledge of nature and history.

In its halls and theaters and lecture rooms, researchers could undertake systematic study. New fields of scholarship were opened. Knowledge began to multiply itself. We took a significant step forward, forever.

This is one of the great world stories, spanning a thousand years.

Of course, up close that big story could be hard to see. There were other stories competing for allegiance. There always are. The city suffered from nearly regular riots throughout its history, one triggered when a soldier killed a slave in an argument over who had the better sandals. Possessions, trade, bickering, political strategizing, and war occupied the minds of many people, then as now.

Local riots and larger wars linked to the rise and fall of empires swept through Alexandria frequently. The library persisted through the comings and goings of Greek, Roman, Christian, and Muslim empires.

The library was partially destroyed over and over by bigotry and war, and finally it was completely destroyed. But the important story is that out of a greedy, ignorant, and violent world, it was built at all. It was built because there were people who wanted knowledge more than profit, understanding more than honor, and clarity more than power. In short, there were people intent on building not a profit-centered community and not a pride-centered community, but an education-centered community.

Stewart Brand (2000) reminded me of this story, and now I've reminded you. If, while reading, you felt promptings to be a little different: to read more, or more carefully, or to be a little more precise in your thinking or a bit more honest in your talking, then you have been influenced by what was done millennia ago. You, too, became a part, however small, of the history of that library. Through its influence on you, its history continues its work among us.

Learning is often a matter of finding, entering, and inhabiting some larger story that gives our lives their meaning. That's how we become members of families and tribes. It's also how we become doctors, jazz musicians, Hell's Angels, farmers, missionaries, and quantum physicists.

CARING FOR LOCAL STORIES

The story of a universal library, having come into the world, has never left. A universal library would include all the world's knowledge and all the people of earth would have access to it. To build such a library will take more than the commitment of our large institutions. It will take the efforts of millions of people in millions of small places, gathering, collecting, and publishing the local knowledge that only they can find and present. People doing heritage projects are small bands of learners and teachers here and there who have learned to see themselves not as spectators and consumers in the great project of human knowledge, but as active participants. They are creating gifts of scholarship, permanent additions to the human record.

Working with schools, museums, libraries, city parks, wildlife refuges, and other community organizations, they document, gather, organize, interpret, create, preserve, and publish the cultural heritage of the localities where they live. A woman may write the biography of her grandfather and place it in the community archives; a retired businessman may write his own life history showing how his personal story is woven through the community's story; and a student might compile an indexed list of obituaries for the local newspaper archive. Most projects are collaborative, involving several individuals or entire classes—and sometimes entire schools—working together to write a history of a farm or a road, to compile the origins of local place names, to gather oral histories of migrants into the locality, to create a species list of a nearby forest, to create a time line charting the establishment and development of local businesses, or to collect local lore on the cultural uses of huckleberries or wild rice.

The present is haunted by people and events now past but not gone, exactly. Our curiosity will reveal aspects of them that they themselves might not have known. We may learn that our true home is not only this shadowed place but also is that company, dimly seen but growing brighter with the years. It begins to matter that our famous fellows— Madison, Sophocles, Lincoln, Paul, Aristotle, and the rest—were here and spoke on issues that still touch us. But it may also matter that others all but unknown were here and did what they did.

The place you now live was given its character by the actions of thousands of people somewhat like Marguerite Greenfield, who once lived near where I live now. The story is told by Joan Bishop (1985) in *Montana the Magazine of Western History*, a publication of the Montana Historical Society. Marguerite started an ice business in Helena, Montana, in 1912 and operated it for twenty-two years. The story of the rise and fall of the Independent Ice Company is a story much like thousands of stories that happened all across America—it's a story of an ordinary person and what she faced, what she attempted, what happened, and how she responded.

Marguerite seemed bored with the routine of managing a household that was a common occupation for women of her standing. She decided to start a business cutting ice in the winter, storing it, then distributing it to people's homes who used it to keep their ice boxes cold in the years before refrigerators. "There is no substitute for ice," she said. "It has got to be delivered. People can burn the piano if they have to, when there is no fuel, but they can't keep the baby's milk sweet with substitutes."

She learned how to use a horse scraper to keep snow off the pond so ice would grow, how to cut twenty-two-inch blocks with a seven-foot ice saw perfectly square and exactly the same size so they fit together tightly, making them less likely to thaw in the storage sheds before they were delivered.

Getting the business started was difficult. Meyer Fish had run the Helena Ice Company for years, and he didn't look kindly upon an upstart competitor—especially a woman moving in on a man's business. He cut his prices. Some people including Marguerite suspected he was behind a series of mysterious accidents at her ice ponds, including a dynamite blast that destroyed her entire ice harvest. He even publicly insinuated that she cut her ice from ponds frequented by ducks.

But Marguerite kept going, her business becoming more profitable every year. Things were going so well that in 1919 Marguerite invested in an ice pond at Elk Creek fifteen miles north of Butte, where the weather was consistently colder than in Helena, so she didn't have to worry any more about winters too warm to grow enough ice. This would also allow her to sell ice to the Great Northern Railway, which used it to cool fruit shipments from Oregon and Washington.

Unfortunately, the railroad system just after World War I was a mess. Right away, the railway division superintendent asked for a bribe—a 35 percent commission, he called it—to guarantee shipments on time.

Marguerite refused. Trains began to pass by her pond without stopping to pick up her ice. Other times the railway crew refused to clear snow off the tracks so trains could get in to load her shipment. Once no train cars moved for ten days while she kept a work crew and horses waiting. Payments for ice the railroad shipped were delayed for months.

Marguerite wrote to the Great Northern headquarters in St. Paul. She was ignored. She wrote to the president of Great Northern Railway. For two months she heard nothing, so she wrote again threatening to go to the newspapers with her story. This motivated the Great Northern to investigate, but they concluded that Marguerite "was not free from the feminine tendency to confuse actual facts with impressions."

So again, nothing happened. Marguerite continued to fight the system. She began keeping careful records of every problem, dates, and details that might hold up in a lawsuit. After years of writing letters, making threats, and battling officials, Marguerite's reports alarmed the Great Northern's legal staff enough that they urged the railroad's president to meet with her and try to appease her.

He surprised Marguerite by listening carefully to her story for three hours. He seemed shocked. "Is there no one honest on my road?" he gasped. The meeting was a success. One official was fired and another was demoted.

Marguerite breathed a sigh of relief and looked forward to making her business prosper. "All I have to do is sell ice," she said.

But by then it was 1931. The Great Depression and drought were wreaking havoc on Montana's economy. New technology was changing everything. Home electric refrigerators and railway refrigerator cars were doing away with the demand for natural ice. In 1933, Marguerite sold only one hundred dollars worth of ice. In 1934 she declared bankruptcy. After years of hope and anger and fighting, Marguerite's business failed. She had never given up, she had refused to deal with corruption, she had fought a good fight.

Ten minutes ago, you had probably never heard of Marguerite Greenfield or thought about how she lived her life. Now you have. Maybe you contemplated the importance of keeping accurate records if you get in a legal tangle. Maybe you thought about how important it is for business owners to be as attentive to technological changes as to day-to-day problems. Maybe you took some courage from her courage. Maybe you thought about the battle she fought between corruption and integrity and leaned toward being on the same side she was on.

If you thought any such thing, then her life became a little more successful than it was just a few minutes ago. By helping you ever so slightly, she makes the world ever so slightly better. Her story has persisted in time, allowing you to experience something of her life.

People sometimes sense something too poignant for words in all this. "The appeal of history to all of us is in the last analysis poetic," says G. M. Trevelyan (as cited in Evans, 1999).

> But the poetry of history does not consist of imagination roaming at large but of imagination pursuing the fact and fastening upon it. That which compels the historian to *scorn delights and live laborious days*, is the ardour of his own curiosity to know what really happened long ago in that land of mystery which we call the past. To peer into that magic mirror and see fresh figures there every day is a burning desire that consumes and satisfies him all his life, that carries him each morning, eager as a lover, to the library and the muniment room. It haunts him like a passion of terrible potency, because it is poetic. The dead were here and are not. Their place knows them no more, and is ours today. Yet they were once as real as we, and we shall tomorrow be shadows like them. . . . The poetry of history lies in the quasi-miraculous fact that once, on this earth, once, on this familiar spot of ground, walked other men and women, as actual as we are today, thinking their own thoughts, swayed by their own passions, but now all gone, one generation vanishing into another, gone as utterly as we ourselves shall shortly be gone, like ghosts at cockcrow.

The attraction we often feel to knowing, simply knowing what it was like for those who were here and now are gone—that attraction is at bottom a hunger for reality. In knowing Marguerite's life we come nearer to knowing our own, and through that knowing she still has a living power to change us, to revise our minds, and, I think, we have the power to change her not by modifying the historical facts of her life but by changing what they mean.

In fascinating ways, the past is not fixed. Arthur Danto (1985) notes that a sentence such as "the Thirty Years War began in 1618" could not have been written in 1618—or in 1628 or in 1638—because no one at those times could see how long the war would last. They could not see vitally important dimensions of what was happening. To give a complete description of the past or the present, we would need a knowledge of all relevant later events. David Weberman (1997) has pointed out that this is something more than a word game. If a man fires a gun at a person at 11:00 a.m. and eight hours later that person dies, the later event, the death, has ontological implications for the earlier event, the pulling of the trigger. The earlier event has changed.

For people alive today, Marguerite Greenfield exists only as a story which we can let play in our consciousness like the music of a newly recovered ancient score. While playing the stories of our predecessors in our minds, we sometimes have visions of the world as we don't want it, and so we move away from some activities. Sometimes we see the world as we do like it, and we move toward that.

Human consciousness is an endless dialogue between past and present, between people now and people then. Always, we are changing each other by learning how the world works and what things mean, how things succeed and how they fail, how they come into existence and how they persist. A group of students that gathers and preserves its community's stories is contributing, in the most fundamental way possible, to the world's educational value. But that's not all. Standing as they do at the beginning of the autobiographical phase of life—the time when they are becoming involved in forming their own identity by turning the events of their own lives into an intelligible story, students have much to learn from studying the actual biographies of family and community elders. The main difference between the stories older teenagers tell about their lives and the stories younger upper elementary students tell, is that high schoolers are leaving behind fantasy and incorporating more and more reality into their stories. This incorporation of reality is the hallmark of maturity. Probably I won't be an NBA star. They cannot hear too many stories about how enterprises start and how they fail, about how people handle sudden good or ill fortune, about people and dreams that collapsed under the pressure of real events and about people and dreams that did not. They are more likely to learn what they need to know by turning the events of actual experience into nonfiction stories than they are by writing so-called creative stories out of their inexperienced imaginations.

Research-based nonfiction writing engages high schoolers in precisely the sort of work they need if they are to fill their powerful minds with what they mostly lack—details of the actual world and experiences of reality. What could be more natural than the pairing of old people who need to reflect on life with young people who need the meat of reality-based stories?

THINKING TOGETHER

With guidance from skilled teachers, high school students doing local research readily find themselves socializing in ways that put them in touch with fundamental questions about the meaning of what they do and who they are. Many students find the experience liberating and energizing. Though they often resist getting started, they like it once they are involved. The work of researching community history in teams feels right. There is a comfort in thinking together. We are made for it. I've sat in rooms where a community's elders talked, with their youth present, about the history of their town—why things happened as they did, which things were mistakes, what might have gone differently, what was worth remembering and admiring. This was done informally, with all the messiness of differing memories and unsystematic disagreements. But the young people nonetheless felt the exhilaration of being brought into the real secrets of adult knowledge, and the older people simply liked the young people: their interest, their optimism, their curiosity, their energy, and their great beauty. The most important work of old age, James Hillman (1999) tells us, is to be an advocate for youth, but when the young and the old lose contact with one another as so often happens today, the old cannot see some of what oldness is for at the same time young people cannot see the horizons of their own humanity.

When we tell young people that it matters that they learn the skills needed to convert ignorance to knowledge, and that they need to learn them by interviewing their elders, collecting scientific data at local ponds and woods, gathering and preserving family stories, investigating occupational cultures, and writing the histories of local organizations and clubs, many of them believe us, and their commitment to learning and discovering and to serving the community doesn't stop with the history of a ranch or a ghost town that they might research and write. They will go on to find solutions for problems we don't yet know are problems because we can't imagine solutions.

The highest achievements of a culture come out of the basic desires of that culture as expressed in the daily habits and practices of its folk-life. A society in which every neighborhood and small town has a baseball team will produce baseball stars capable of amazing feats. We have yet to develop a culture of scholarship where the work of original research and discovery isn't the privilege of a small class of specialists but is part of the lives of nearly everyone. But we will create such a culture as we become increasingly bored with lesser pursuits, and when we do that culture will transcend the cultures we are familiar with in somewhat the way cultures of literacy transcend those where people do not have contracts or accounts or blueprints or books.

Today, something like the Library at Alexandria is coming within reach of everyone who lives on earth. We have for the first time the technical means to put the power of knowledge within reach of all the earth's peoples, which means we have a chance to revisit all our old stories. We can join the story of ourselves providing the gifts of knowledge of medicine, governance, agriculture, religion, literature, art, and science to all the peoples on earth, if understanding ourselves as part of that story is what we desire. It's an intelligent desire.

We are flooded with information and this can disorient us, letting us forget that knowledge is as compelling a human need as food and water. The peasants crowded into cathedrals in the Middle Ages, praying for deliverance from the bubonic plague that was killing millions, killing so many they could not be buried, so that dogs ran through city streets carrying human heads in their mouths, were suffering from a lack of knowledge. They did not know what was happening or what they should do. They were oblivious to the fleas leaping among them, carrying the disease from person to person.

If we are to do more with our new communication technologies than build the world's largest shopping mall and spy on one another, which we will do in any case, we need to teach the generation now in school that the work for this age is the great unfinished project of human knowledge, and that by joining their efforts together, they can accomplish something heroic, something worthy of their natural idealism. They can take the Library at Alexandria to a new level, helping all the people of the earth and all the future generations.

They like to know they are taking part in a heroic quest such as the worldwide heritage project. But that, by itself, isn't enough. They also need people near at hand. Students have told me repeatedly that what was most important to them about their heritage projects were the relationships in the here and now: the joy of working with a small team of fellow student researchers, the chance to get to know personally older people in the community, and the chances to go places and do things as members of a group. In this, our youth are not so different from us. These are the things that bring us joy as well.

It is critical that we teach the generation now in school that they are not mere recipients of the great project of human knowledge but active participants in it. We can best teach them this by participating ourselves—not just those of us who are professional teachers, but those of us who are nurses or cowboys or grandmothers or accountants or gardeners.

Most of the world's knowledge is not in the Library of Congress or the Centers for Disease Control and Prevention. It's spread throughout the planet, in communities built and sustained by ordinary people. We all know that digital publishing makes the local library an outlet for the world's knowledge, but equally important, it invites each local library to become an input point for the world's knowledge about the particular locality where that library is situated. If you do not gather the history and lore and geography of your ancestors and of your place, who will do it?

Some people see this. Good work has been done by many cultural adventurers such as Hal Cannon at the Western Folklore Center with his Deep West Project. Others are finding it out through such websites as YouTube. Amidst all the flotsam are videos far more interesting than the latest episode of a network sitcom. As we learn more, the quality of the storytelling about our own lives will increase. We will do amazing things with the insight that today we have the wealth and leisure to see that every community has its own great library—not just a collection of books, but also a gathering of people, some young and some old, at all levels of learning, not just taking knowledge away from the library, but bringing new knowledge there.

As a people, we have excelled at creating large-scale, centralized systems of governance, entertainment, manufacturing, marketing, and education. We now realize this has often led us to neglect our communities and neighborhoods. We see that it is also through the work of local culture that we shape our destiny. Self-determination is never going to be achieved by begging for it from centralized power. It will be achieved by local communities applying their intelligence to the places they live, asking where they are, who they are, what is worthy of their desire, and what they can responsibly do to attain it.

"Personal experience is the soul of a town," wrote high school student Desarae Baker from Simms, Montana, as she meditated on the history her class was working on of buildings that have fallen down and are rotting away in her dying rural village. She noted sadly that such places "are part of [people's] knowledge of each other." Her study and reflection have brought her to the realization that as the buildings vanish, so do features of our minds and our relationships.

Every family, neighborhood, and community would benefit from having thoughtful members writing and preserving their histories, asking such questions as these: What has happened here? Where are we now? What capacities and abilities do we have? What can we do to take care of ourselves and our place? These are questions groups can ask and answer at the level of family, neighborhood, town, and region.

After repairing a fence his grandfather built, high school student Zeb Engstrom from the small prairie town of Chester, Montana, paused to write about what it meant. "The barrier of time between me and the man who built it thinned and shimmered in the summer heat . . . I can almost feel the old hired hands sitting around the stove in the bunkhouse telling jokes and stories, and the air smells faintly of the soup that boiled on the stove," he said.

It moved him to see himself as taking his place in a larger picture, wanting to make himself a strong link in the chain of generations. "It was on that day that I stopped complaining about fixing fence or building buildings. Without my grandpa's work and my dad's work, my life would be a lot harder."

Young people like Desarae and Zeb are helping create a local literature, based on local history, local folkways, local geography, and local science. While the world of official education is quite noisy with the commotion caused by new testing regimes, a grassroots revolution has been developing for decades that moves to different music. It goes by many names—service learning, civic education, place-based instruction, character education, and community-centered teaching. What these approaches have in common is that they conceive of education as being linked to work in the real world, they place great importance on developing relationships, and they do so by forming communities of purpose. They focus on engaging students with places, with communities, and with life outside the school. In a world where better stories eventually supplant weaker ones, the force that Machiavelli called fortune and that St. Paul called providence and that I will simply call history will ensure that education will become increasingly personal, increasingly caring, and will succeed by inviting students to join communities of purpose ordered around larger goals than individual career success.

The first step is to build those communities of purpose.

CHAPTER 5

Education and Community

Man cannot stand alone in the face of eternity: he needs the comfort of purpose, the peace of forgiveness, and the confidence of truth.

—Eric S. Cohen

WHICH STORIES?

Since communities form around shared stories, the first step in thinking about how to make communities better may be to think about what makes stories good. That different groups in society have different answers to this question is, of course, one of the central difficulties of our age. John Dewey (1916) wrestled with a similar problem. He was casting about for criteria by which to judge which communities were good or bad, because he had noted that when we look at our actual communities we find "men banded together in a criminal conspiracy, business aggregations that prey upon the public while serving it, political machines held together by the interest of plunder." But even in the worst of these we still find characteristics we want to say we are looking for, such as "loyalty" and "common purpose."

"There is honor among thieves," he said, "and a band of robbers has a common interest as respects its members. Gangs are marked by fraternal feeling, and narrow cliques by intense loyalty to their own codes."

He decided that thinking about "the amount of interaction and cooperative intercourse with other groups" might serve as a criterion. The number of other organizations that criminal groups communicate with freely is quite limited, and the number of things individual gang members have in common with one another is often not much more than a shared desire to plunder. In other words, he thought more relationship was better.

This seems precisely the right direction. It is the criterion of life itself. Life is developing relationships, elaborating higher and higher states of order by establishing more and more complex webs of communication. Ecosystems move from a few pioneering plants, supporting a few herbivores, and even fewer predators, to the enormously complicated systems within systems within systems of a mature forest, and as they do, the amount of information that is moving between and within organisms, species, and communities continues increasing.

For years I've directed a rural volunteer ambulance service. One can see some aspects of life quite clearly by watching the way death undoes a living person. Death is a process of separations, frayings, and unravelings. Carefully tuned relationships between systems start getting out of whack. The first symptom of trouble is a loss of alertness. Alertness itself isn't a single thing but a network of relationships through which we are precisely attuned to our environment. An alert person knows who he is, where he is, when he is, and what is happening, and this knowing requires a fabulous hierarchy of systems and subsystems constantly interacting through elaborate feedback loops. Information in the form of electricity and chemicals flows from all the levels through all the other levels: systems, organs, tissues, cells. Scientists have worked for decades to unravel the sophistication just of communication strategies that go on below the level of cells.

In a dying person, alertness goes first. Then, if the disturbance of disease or trauma isn't removed, the body becomes too unstable to sustain personality and, later, even consciousness is lost. If nothing is done, the unraveling continues. A beating heart receives a message from higher in the system in the form of an electric impulse that causes millions of cardiac cells to act in coordination. This vast coordination of processes results in the cells contracting in unison, and their unified actions create a muscular squeezing that forces blood from the heart chambers. When the communication becomes disorganized, the relationship between cells is lost. Each reverts to an individual rhythm and continues contracting on its own for a few minutes. Now instead of beating the heart quivers in an ineffective, dying state that we call "ventricular fibrillation" but that the French more vividly call "ventricular anarchy."

When the heart stops, the body goes on dying for hours. Nerve cells die in minutes, while muscle cells die in hours. Some anaerobic processes continue for many hours, but one by one, isolated cells go still and silent.

If life is an ultimate locus of value, and I believe it is, then it would seem reasonable to follow Dewey in thinking that one criterion by which we can judge stories is the manner in which the stories portray relationships. Those that promote more and stronger relationships are better than those that undermine or weaken relationships. Good stories partake of life by increasing relationship, and bad stories advance death by garbling relationships. Of course, applying this criterion without regard to the subtleties or mysteries through which stories move could lead to a dull-witted, flat-footed insistence on the proper didactic message as the test of a story's worth. This criterion also leaves aside the entire realm of technical beauty, including such things as management of suspense, vividness of description, elegance of language, and much more. Still, it seems clear that some stories are on the side of death and others are on the side of life, and that we are shaped by which we choose. If we want to, we can learn better methods for governing ourselves, progressing from governments based on fear, to those organized around law, to those motivated by love. We need, then, stories that help us see ourselves in larger and larger contexts. In an essay I published a few years ago, I offered this formulation: "A story that leads me to take delight in caring for my family is better than one that encourages me to look out only for myself, and one that tempts me to care for the welfare of the whole tribe is better than one that suggests my obligations end with my family, and one that shows me how to feel compassion for all of humanity is better than one that leads me to think of outsiders as enemies, and one that instills a reverence for all of creation is about as good as stories get."

A good school needs to be organized around good stories, and few stories seem as useful for educators as the story of our growing understanding, through history, of what makes a good community. It's a story that has real implications for every student since all young people crave more or better relationships. We all need to live in good communities or we can't satisfy ourselves bodily, emotionally, spiritually, and intellectually.

As we try to understand community better, we find ourselves facing both practical and philosophical questions, and we discover that all academic disciplines have light to shed upon them. Furthermore, examples of communities are readily available for study in literature and history as well as in journalism and the social sciences. Even better, local communities exist near at hand, accessible for original research by students. And since the actual community that surrounds and interpenetrates the school will always be an intersection between many things, the scene where all our disquiets come to a head and where all our confusions are met, there need be nothing limiting or parochial about a focus upon local community.

A conscious decision to put community at the center of schooling makes sense for several reasons. The sociologist Elijah Anderson (1990) argues that as we leave behind the vital sense of community that once brought the young and the old together, we begin to suffer from "cultural amnesia." In strong communities, the young were helped to grow up by wise elders—"old heads," Anderson calls them—who acted as "a kind of guidance counselor and moral cheerleader."

Children met these old heads in small jobs, at church, in school, or simply on the street corner. The old head might be a police officer, a favorite teacher, or a grocer. The old heads took interest in the community's young people, and the young responded with ready deference. For children without available fathers and mothers, the old heads were sources of consolation, advice, occasional help (including financial), and, above all, sources of moral values well laced with doses of real-life wisdom.

Young people would hang around at odd places "to listen to his witty conversation and moral tales of hard work and decency. They truly felt that they were learning something worthwhile from someone they could look up to and respect. One of the primary messages of the old head was about good manners and the value of hard work: how to dress for a job interview and deal with a prospective employer, how to work, and how to keep the job. Through stories, jokes, and conversations, the old head would convey his conception of the 'tricks of the trade.'"

This sort of informal education doesn't happen as often or as easily as it once did. Individual entertainments, such as television and the Internet, keep us from meeting as regularly in public spaces. William Damon (1990), a psychologist at Brown University, notes that intergenerational sharing is threatened as "skepticism and rebelliousness replace respect for authority, and guile replaces social responsibility." No doubt such trends are real.

But as Rene Dubos (1972) reminded us years ago, "trend is not destiny." At a community pageant produced by students of Marta Brooks at St. Ignatius High School, high school seniors had interviewed members of the community who were eighty years old or older. They had worked their life stories into a dramatic script modeled on Edgar Lee Masters' book, *Spoon River Anthology*. The elders were in the audience, along with other family members, and the youngsters performed their stories.

The elders talked about all sorts of things, but since they knew they were speaking for the public record and to young people, they tended to put their best faces on. Several themes were repeated so often that little doubt remained that these were understandings that the older Montanans wanted the next generation to believe.

First, family is more important than money or careers. In their own life stories as they chose to tell them, the elders made it clear that jobs come and go, careers are interrupted or abandoned, the economy changes, but through it all we can find solace and joy in our relationships with parents, brothers, sisters, children, and grandchildren. If the evening had a unifying theme, this was it.

Second, hard work "works." The elders told the town's youth, not in sermons but through stories of their lives, that the traditional virtues of diligence, thrift, persistence, and reliability had allowed them to overcome hardship and sometimes severe poverty. Looking back over sixty or seventy years of effort, the elders saw quite clearly that practicing such virtues had allowed them to increase the abundance in their lives—to have good food, good housing, a solid business, a productive garden, or a tight barn. There seemed an especial fondness for talking about the bad times because these were the times, as in a difficult ball game, when their strengths were most clearly on display. They took great satisfaction in gazing back over years of steady, productive effort.

And finally, neighborliness was evident as a crucial virtue both for dealing with sudden misfortune and for filling life with pleasure. Lettie Kent Pierce Gilbert told of a doctor breaking the windshield out of his Model A so he could see to get to her during a raging blizzard. Arvil Anderson told of the symphony orchestra that came and performed on his front yard to honor his work as a maker of fine violins (he made them in the evenings, after his day work as a potato farmer was finished). The good life can't be lived in isolation. We are in this together, the elders seemed to be saying to their youth.

Morality, as Wendell Berry (1989) suggests, is long-term practicality, and most places have elders who have figured out what works. This isn't to say that all elders have become wise or even that they are all good people. But the more we see them as sources of wisdom rather than as obsolete careerists, the more wise they tend to become.

TOWARD EDUCATION-CENTERED COMMUNITIES

Robert Bellah et al. (1991) observes that "education can never merely be for the sake of individual self-enhancement. It pulls us into a common world or it fails altogether." Education is our general term for all the related processes of finding out what works and passing it on to others, and as the biologists repeat endlessly, this is the basic process of life.

I'm speaking of communities primarily in the sense of geographical towns and neighborhoods which are felt by their members to be communities, but much of what I say is also true in a very broad sense for any human institution that people form deliberately to accomplish work that individuals can't accomplish alone. The etymology for "community," "commonwealth," "commonality," "communication," and "communion" leads us to the Latin idea of "with mutual duties." If any group of people believes they have formed a community, I'm disinclined to quibble with them over definitions. For present purposes, a more precise definition may not help much, since the point is not to describe actual communities so much as to encourage people to act with others to advance shared purposes.

The important understandings are that communities require deliberate action and freedom on the part of their members, and that the members think together to accomplish mutual goods. Communities are formed and kept together by free individuals. It may seem that people had no choice about being members of traditional hunter-gatherer communities, but in fact most such groups allowed people to leave whenever they wanted. Few people chose to leave because their chances outside the community were quite grim. Today, the consequences of living outside a community are less likely to include physical starvation, but we learn more every year about other ways we suffer by being isolated. Some towns succeed quite well as communities and others do not. Making a town or a neighborhood or a school work better as a community requires that people want it to be so and that they are willing to act on behalf of their desire.

Communities have at least three other attributes that are worth pondering. First, they are relaxed in some ways even when they are tensed to meet crises. The relaxation has to do with the understanding that whatever happens, the members will stay together. The tacit understanding is that at a level deeper than our disagreements, we're basically okay with each other. Sure, there are problems to be solved, but that's not really a problem. That's just life. That's why we're here.

Second, good communities constantly turn problems into common work that people can share. In fact, the main joy of being in a community may stem from the reality that work is something we can share. Compared to work, pleasure is quite private and in many ways isolating. People are forever trying to make relationships strong by basing them on shared pleasure, but most often they will have more success by basing them on shared work. The pleasure will happen along the way, like the noon meal on cattle branding day.

And third, communities create a gift-based economy. They create a form of grace, where we don't earn everything we get. We don't earn the beautiful streets and peaceful parks, the free schools, the library card, the chance to join a volleyball league, the safe water, or the passerby who stops when our car breaks down. Though we want to contribute, to add our own gifts to the buffet, we can never put in as much as we get back. Gifford Pinchot (1995) points out that the entire enterprise of human knowledge, itself a communal enterprise, is a gift economy. "At a symposium, a scientist *gives* a paper. If scientists followed the rules of an exchange economy, scientists would not give papers; they would seek to get a good deal by selling them or trading them in such a way that they got more knowledge than they gave. They would gain status not by giving away knowledge but by hoarding it. If scientists followed the rules of the exchange economy we might not have escaped the Dark Ages." The greatest teacher is not the one who possesses the most knowledge but the one who has managed one way or another to give the most away.

It's possible, maybe even easy, to move into a town or a neighborhood and live there without joining a community. This is especially true in towns and cities that have allowed the exchange economy to all but destroy the gift economy. I recently spent a few days in downtown Portland, Oregon. Outside, I walked the streets of a profit-centered community. I could get good food, pleasant drinks, and sit in sumptuous surroundings, as long as I was buying something. Everywhere I turned, commercial messages bombarded me, trying to get me to spend money on this or that. The place was noisy with the bustle of selling. Since I'm not much of a shopper, the busy streets that seemed so interesting on first glance soon became monotonous. More shops selling purple soap on ropes and incense holders and thousands of things to dust. Even though I was on an expense account, I had the gnawing sense that I was hemorrhaging money.

Eventually, I found the Oregon Historical Society's museum. Grateful for respite, I walked in from the busy street and spent a couple hours examining exhibits. When I left, I chose the door on the opposite side of the building from where I entered. Only a block away from the busy commercial district, I found myself in a park—a green and peaceful place, one kind of an education-centered community. Instead of shops selling cigars, earrings, purses, movie tickets, and strong coffee, I stood before an expanse of grass, trees, and statues. It was surrounded with benches, where people sat for free, nobody trying to peddle them anything. Others sat conversing. A young couple sat very close, looking each other full in the face from time to time, talking. Their three-year-old girl played nearby. Costly buildings lined the way: churches, art galleries, and museums. People came and went, mostly in small groups rather than as solitary individuals, which was more common only a block away. I began to feel refreshed.

Most towns have sections that are built less to make money than to preserve and present what we know of truth, beauty, and goodness. Such places let us glimpse a future that is ours for the wanting. To be sure, that education-centered street in Portland was paid for with activities undertaken for profit. It was a gift the people gave themselves. The point is not that we need to get by without politics or profits, but only that we need to guard against them looming larger in our lives than is good for us. We are building vast expanses of fast-food stores, drive-in banks, convenience stores, shopping plazas, and gasoline stations where one can wander amid the noise for hours, or days, or perhaps a lifetime without finding anything good to read or anyone with enough time and interest for a good conversation.

Our spirits cry for more. In my consulting work in schools, I've had discussions across the nation with people who are hungry to read and talk and write and create. Working in small towns such as Nevada City, Nevada, or in large cities such as New Orleans, they are quietly and steadily developing their sense of place and their sense of time by focusing on doing intellectual and cultural work aimed at better understanding their particular geographical localities. They are forming and joining education-centered communities by engaging in heritage projects.

Such heritage projects provide a glimpse of a possible future. We can make any community more education centered. Education-centered communities still have restaurants and hotels and banks and gas stations. And they still have political parties and elections. Psychologists still try to understand the mind and how to help people with troubles. There are still plenty of people who need help. Poverty, disease, and ignorance still tax us. We still pursue our deepest learning with people who share our religious and cultural beliefs. But fewer people try to create an identity by buying the right shoes or furniture, fewer people wait for distant institutions to solve local problems, fewer people think pleasure provides enough structure to organize a life, and fewer people fear linking arms with those who are different from them, to walk together as far as possible.

People retire when they can afford to and volunteer at museums and libraries. Wealthy people donate large sums to the ongoing work of creating, gathering, preserving, organizing, and presenting local knowledge.

Writers, scientists, curators, and other knowledge workers find people eager to help them. And young people find lots of ways to join groups of adults doing real work.

More and more schools recognize that if they are not embedded in strong communities they cannot do a good job. This is becoming a refrain among educators. Craig B. Howley et al. (1996) express a set of understandings that is becoming more and more widespread. Beginning with the insight that "the good upbringing of children is a community endeavor," Howley et al. point out that schooling "according to the massive urban model fails," because "it cannot call on community." Community, they say, "has been lost in a mobile urban society." In mass society, the mission of schooling becomes "impersonal and distant" and operates to extract schooling "from its cultural roots and to extract it from the context that permits true education to flourish." This has led to urgent pleas for educators "to invent communities to compensate for what has been lost."

In a similar vein, Paul Theobald and Jim Curtiss (2000) suggest that "the quality of human community in this country has suffered enormous damage, and, as a result, we have tried to bureaucratize and institutionalize the solution to our cultural shortcomings. That is, we have tried to create 'all-purpose' schools." But, they add, "to appreciably attend to the 'needs' of students, schools must contribute to the re-creation of communities."

Schools can most powerfully contribute to the re-creation of communities by providing a center around which people can gather. Education is everyone's business. Education matters to kids in education-centered communities because it matters to adults. Learning is not a chore of youth but a central meaning of existence, and people from all walks of life remain engaged in teaching and learning. Teachers do not face large groups of children alone, but are joined often by parents, elders, and the staffs of other community organizations.

It isn't hard to envision a community that is not politics centered, profit centered, or pride centered but education centered. In such a community, people commit a portion of their resources to forming a better understanding of the world in all its aspects and of making gifts to the community of that understanding. Our communities are full of institutions brought into existence for just such reasons. They include museums, libraries, action committees, galleries, parks, research hospitals, book groups, nonprofit associations, businesses, historical societies, wildlife refuges, and churches, to name a few.

Many such institutions have active outreach programs, which is their name for educational initiatives, and most see that their future is dependent upon teaching young people what they do and why it matters. The school is the natural center through which these institutions can forge the relationships needed to develop to higher levels.

CHAPTER 6

Teaching as a Craft of Place

The education agenda that over the years has shifted from a local concern to a state and national one must, in part, return to a local focus. The curriculum must grow out of real issues important to the students and the people in a particular community. Activities that connect with one's own experience, that require the use of skills from various disciplines, that are carried out in cooperation with others, and that result in a useful product give students the most powerful kinds of learning experiences.

—Paul Theobald

As teachers and community members begin looking anew at their schools and communities, asking what they can do together to make life in the community more rich, a process of renewal unfolds, in which, as Toni Haas and Paul Natchtigal (1998) say, "long-standing needs become opportunities for collaboration and learning." As the work proceeds, "resources are uncovered, redefined, and invested in new ways." And fundamental strengths are revitalized, including the "capacity to support social relationships, to anchor community life, to keep students close to home and rooted in their culture, and to give identity to communities."

The training that teachers receive helps them to think of themselves less as members of local communities than of professional associations, and all sorts of organizations would like to control schools from Washington, D.C., in no small part because the contracts to disseminate programs would be stunningly lucrative. Such actualities put steady pressure on schools to become local franchises of national programs.

Teachers doing heritage projects often see that education suffers when it's completely divorced from efforts to live well in the particular—that is, local—places the students know. Like gardening, sailing, and politics, teaching is a craft of place. Though gardeners learn quite a lot from botany texts, it is the challenge of raising particular plants in particular places that draws them into their liveliest encounters with books. Similarly, good sailors know quite a lot about geography, meteorology, and physics because such knowledge forms the context within which they work and play, but these subjects are compelling mostly because the outcome of actual—that is, local—encounters with land and sea and weather depend upon applied knowledge. And good politicians often have heads full of history because such knowledge is a practical necessity to deal with real—that is, local—situations. All politics, we have heard, is local. So in an important sense is all learning. Newton could see the force that held the solar system in order by observing particular—that is, local—apples falling, and Einstein could imagine the curving of the universe by contemplating that universe from his vantage point on a particular—that is, local—lake in Switzerland.

Students in a civics class who attempt to think more clearly and more deeply about a current political controversy, such as a school bond election, by collecting oral histories about a similar event in the community's past—getting a bond passed to build the gymnasium in 1972, for example—and compare what they are told in such interviews with newspaper accounts written at the time may begin understanding the nuances of how such things work. They experience for themselves the ways communities enact themselves and individuals fulfill themselves by entering the public arena where shared purposes are negotiated. Both history and theory begin to come to life. They will also learn quite a lot about how to read newspapers—how contrived the reality presented there actually is. And by inviting community elders to reflect on past events, they can bring perspective to the adults involved in the current community discussion.

Students in a biology class who assist refuge managers in collecting data on insect population fluctuations begin to see how scientific knowledge is constructed through methodical effort. As the students participate, they begin to see changes that can only be seen by keeping records. They may begin to consider changes they want and changes they don't want.

Classrooms that never use academic work to accomplish tasks in the real world are somewhat like football teams that drill and scrimmage endlessly but never play games. It becomes difficult for all involved to remember why standards matter or what the point of the busyness might be.

Students doing heritage projects have assisted libraries and museums in building their oral history collections and in improving their historical photograph archives; they have done field archaeology and data collection for state natural resource agencies; they have assisted local people in completing the research to nominate community buildings to the National Register of Historic Places; they have created audio tours for local museums; and they have compiled histories of local organizations. Such projects allow students to gain crucial skills at the same time they accomplish work that benefits the community.

Such projects also draw ever-expanding circles of other community members to the work. In February 1997 at the Montana Historical Society when Montana governor Marc Racicot talked to a meeting of teachers doing heritage projects, including one in the governor's hometown of Libby, he noted that the projects of collecting, preserving, and presenting a community's cultural heritage could be understood as a contemporary form of barn raising—a shared enterprise that binds people together by giving them a common purpose. People gather because there is work to do. Afterward, they remember most vividly the good times.

It's hard to overstate how much fun it can be to discover the lost worlds of the past. I've gone with teams of high school students to an abandoned cemetery they discovered in the woods, where the first fur trader in the area is buried with his Indian family, near a vanished fort. I've accompanied a team of students to Lewis and Clark campsites that they located after weeks of research, using journals and GPS software, so they could document the present, comparing the flora and fauna with the 1804 journals. I've camped with a class of high school students at an abandoned gold mining town—about which the kids had become the world's leading authorities—where they were completing a field archaeology project, to write the history of a place that had been all but forgotten.

Consequences of such work ripple through the school and community, offering hopeful answers to many community questions: How can we involve our youth in serving others? How can we smooth the transition from school to work by providing experiences in out-of-classroom settings? How can we give young people a sense of belonging? How can we make the curriculum relevant to contemporary concerns? How can we encourage greater parent and community involvement in the schools?

It isn't necessary or even advisable that heritage projects replace all other schoolwork. Traditional teaching has an important role to play in any young person's education. What *is* advisable is to balance and enliven abstract curricula with local applications. If teachers would engage their local communities, they would find that often they are engaging their students as well. It would be good if every student could have at least one class each term that dealt directly and intensively with local knowledge or local issues. If every class could spend a part of the school year focusing on local issues, helping students find personal connection to stories larger than themselves, seeing the ways individuals are intertwined with communities and communities with states and with nations, both the world and school might make more sense.

As young people become more aware of local crises and dilemmas, their investigations can furnish them with ideas about what choices are possible. They find evidence of the consequences of various ways of thinking and acting. They become more likely to make intelligent choices.

Adults doing real work face the limits of knowledge regularly and they are keenly aware that human knowledge is an unfinished project, but this is harder for students to see. They look forward to year after year in classrooms where knowledge seems finished, where it seems that someone else has already figured out everything. It can be hard to believe that their efforts matter, except for careerist reasons. Does the world really need them?

At the local level, the limits of human knowledge are near at hand. What is the frog population of Mission Creek this year compared with last year? Where did the bricks to build that old Mission Church come from? When we bring young people with us in our quests to know our home better, we teach them how worlds are made, why knowledge matters, and what we need to know that we do not yet know. We also enjoy one another.

As best we can, we pass on the craft of living well.

LEADING BY TEACHING

Communities that become more education centered usually do so in response to schools that have become more community centered. Schools can be powerful forces in the revitalization of the neighborhoods and communities where they are located. Watching teachers who begin heritage projects, I've been intrigued by how often they become powerful community leaders, not by attending town council meetings or political coffees, but by providing opportunities for people to get involved. They practice an invitational style of leadership—leading by starting some work and then by crafting invitations. People who won't show up for yet another planning meeting or visioning session or training workshop will come when invited to help kids do some real project. Do I want to come to a school board meeting to discuss curriculum? Not really. Will I come tell the kids what I know about the 1964 floods? Yes, and I'll bring my photo album and newspaper clippings. More often than not, they'll find they liked it. They'll come again when asked again, and they'll tell other people it's a good thing.

Teachers doing heritage projects lead by becoming, in William Purkey's phrase, more "personally and professionally inviting" (Purkey and Stanley, 1989). They lead by caring and by asking for help. Humanity's greatest leaders have always been teachers—people who show another way. The pattern holds true in towns and cities today. A learning community is creativity in motion, bringing knowledge and relationships that did not exist before into being. Those working together on heritage projects move into unmapped terrain, relying on compasses more than on maps, staying oriented by holding in mind the general direction and the big questions that are being considered. The issue is less "What's the plan?" than "What's the story?" What's moving, changing, and living? Who are we becoming?

Four principles, optimism, trust, respect, and intentionality, can help in crafting invitations for specific people.

Optimism: People are attracted to and changed by those who act confidently on behalf of a good future. People are goal-seeking creatures, and the goals they seek are shaped by what they believe they face. Optimists tap into the principle of power that draws people toward what they desire. Resources are more likely to flow toward them.

Trust: The first lesson in learning how to swim is to relax and float, learning to trust that the water will hold us up. People are most effective when they are somewhat relaxed, trusting that in general things will work out. To take action in a changing world, we need to move beyond what is obvious and safe. This is easier when we recognize that occasional losses can be absorbed. We aren't going to drown. Relaxed, we can direct our attention away from the shortcomings of others and toward building trust by being trustworthy ourselves: honest, dependable, cheerful, and generous.

Respect: We can't accomplish much by ourselves, and we can't enlist much help without respecting the abilities and intentions of others. So to get much done, we need to respect others. When you begin asking people—especially old people—about their life experiences, you will inevitably be astonished by some people who appear quite ordinary. Most elderly people have lived through experiences that surprise younger people. Your students will be even more astonished than you will be. One of the things students doing heritage projects comment on over and over is how fascinating older people become when someone simply takes the time to ask about their lives and then to listen. Repeatedly, they say it changes their lives. It certainly changes the attitudes of community members toward young people and toward schools.

As we cultivate the habit of respect, we learn more and more how capable many other people are of taking initiative and acting upon events rather than being acted upon by them. We come to trust that they have reasons and intelligence of their own, and possibilities often emerge that are better than what would have happened if we had simply got our way.

Intentionality: Good classes and good schools always have an air of intentionality about them. They don't happen accidentally. Intentionality binds past, present, and future into meaningful stories. When we act intentionally, we are forward looking, acting in the present, using each moment to advance in desired directions, bringing will and commitment to the making of a story that is really so.

Teachers leading heritage projects open ways for people beyond the classroom to work together on such communal creations as a museum exhibit involving a dozen people's talents, a book of local history essays, a heritage festival, a mentoring program, or a local history trail with interpretive signs.

Such projects succeed through a thousand small interactions. Sociologists who have studied social capital, the web of networks and relationships that undergird strong towns and neighborhoods, have become more and more aware of the way that groups prepare themselves for large accomplishments—building hospitals and schools or fostering economic development—by getting to know one another in simpler endeavors.

"I am done with great things and big plans," says the pioneering psychologist William James (1926). "I am for those tiny, invisible loving human forces that work from individual to individual, creeping through the crannies of the world like so many rootlets, or like the capillary oozing of water, yet which, if given time, will rend the hardest monuments of human pride."

Schools have proven to be quite resilient to improvement by directives from afar, and a growing number of educators are coming to see such directives as much of the problem. People who are in place, caring about one another and their situation, have changed the world in the past and will do so in the future.

What we most need are not directives but invitations, and not from afar but from near at hand.

COMMUNITY SELF-STUDY

At the beginning of his heritage project a few years ago, Jeff Gruber asked his high school civics class to send letters of invitation and placed stories in the local newspaper asking adults to join them in a study of their community.

In an upstairs room at the local bank, with white marker boards, stacking chairs, and folding tables, more than thirty citizens, including the mayor, a forest service archaeologist, church and business leaders, and a city council member, joined forces with high school seniors in the evenings to conduct an intensive ten-week community self-study. They intended to follow a study guide, *Life in Montana*, published fifty years before as part of the Montana Study, a community development program developed by Ernest Melby, chancellor of the University of Montana, and funded by the Rockefeller Foundation.

The Montana Study came into existence during the depths of World War II, when the future of American democracy itself seemed uncertain. For Ernest Melby, a follower of John Dewey, democracy was inseparable from education. He challenged people in Montana towns to improve their lives using education as their primary tool. He was sure that if people joined together to study and discuss their communities, they would find their way forward.

However, they weren't allowed to solve any problems—at least not at first. Trying to solve problems would quickly lead into familiar debates. Melby was after something better: a community organized around the pursuit of insight and understanding. A time for solving problems would come later, after time was spent developing the educated habits of withholding judgment, looking for evidence, analyzing information, resolving differences of opinion through further research, and listening to one another.

Through practicing self-education, the community could move beyond politics-centered debating to the more powerful work of shared inquiry. Melby (1959) was confident that local communities had to do this work themselves. "If we examine the problems confronting modern society," he said, "we find that the vast majority of them are essentially problems in human relations. The problems of world peace, of satisfactory industrial relations, of juvenile delinquency, of bad housing, of race relations and of religious conflicts—all these come to a head in the community. In their solution people must be brought together and there must be mutual acceptance, conversation and collaboration. All of them are difficult to teach by word of mouth. Nearly always we like people better when we really get to know them."

Education needed to be enacted in the community, he believed, rather than implemented at the school. "No curriculum change in our educational system, at any or all levels of schools and colleges, is going to give us the faith we need," Melby (1959) said, "unless it is coupled with a vitalized community which in its everyday life is exemplifying the attitudes we need and giving people the educational opportunities they should have. In other words, an education-centered community is a vital requisite for the building of an educational program that will renew our faith in freedom."

When Art Ortenberg decided to fund the Montana Heritage Project through the Liz Claiborne and Art Ortenberg Foundation, he offered the Montana Study as a model to think about. The story of the Montana Study was nearly fifty years old but it hadn't lost its power to make new people think. It was this story that got several teachers thinking about education-centered communities at about the time my work as a high school principal had led me to think that as long as our schools were politically governed, the entire community was going to have to be the unit of educational improvement. What Melby meant by an "education-centered community" goes far beyond what most school people understand as community involvement. Often it doesn't mean anything beyond some public relations, with the school sending out positive messages hoping to make people feel good about what's going on. Melby called this the first level of community involvement.

At the second level, he said, parents begin helping out as aides and people begin paying attention to how the school runs. Maybe they go to school board meetings and wait for their three minutes at the microphone.

The real excitement for Melby (1959) began at the third level, at "the moment a community begins to see itself as a whole and begins to undertake its own development and its own education." Now instead of just reacting to what happens, people are "taking the first step to reach the third level in community involvement for schools, the level we have chosen to call the *education-centered community*. Here the assumption is that people cannot be educated by others."

Melby argued that education isn't something we have or that others do to us, it is something we do. Just as "each of us individually must educate himself, so with the community as a whole. If the community only recognizes how education takes place and realizes that we learn by doing, by involvement, by participation, and begins to organize itself with educational objectives in mind—at that moment it puts itself in position to begin to use its resources."

When a group of people begins asking the basic question, what do we need to learn and do to make this town a better place to live for all of us, for all of the groups and families that are here, and for all of our children, then "for the first time voluntary associations, schools, newspapers, radio stations, churches, and civic groups of all kinds begin to fall into place. The school is no longer the one and only educational enterprise in the community. It is a means utilized by the community for its own education. Moreover, it is utilized along with other agencies to achieve generally accepted community purposes."

Melby (1959) thought that if we were going to stop fighting and begin learning and teaching, we had to "have something outside us and beyond us that can serve as the focus of our affections. People who think only of themselves have bad mental health. People who seek only money and power wind up poor in things of the spirit. Our tradition of freedom, respect for individual human beings, and human brotherhood gives each of us, as well as our nation, something to live for, something 'outside us and beyond us' to which we can give ourselves."

The Montana Study was modeled after even older stories—those of New England town meetings in which people came together in study groups to examine their own lives in their own towns. A different discussion leader guided the group each week. Each week the group listened to research reports by some members and then used this research as the basis of further discussion. Structure was provided by their guidebook, *Life in Montana*, which led them through a series of research projects, such as creating histories of schools, businesses, and churches; analyzing the ways people fulfilled their needs for recreation; studying the way the town fit into regional and national economic patterns; tracing changes caused by modern life; examining the effects of migration in and out; and so on.

In most cases, communities that completed study groups went on to take action based on the recommendations of the various committees that were formed during the ten-week study. In Libby, the group went on to build a gymnasium for the school.

Jeff Gruber had his students read chapters from *Small Town Renaissance* (Poston, 1950), a history of the Montana Study. "We discussed reasons for studying one's community," he said. "And a different way of learning, one that would take place out of the classroom, without text books, worksheets, or tests. It sounded strange, but also interesting, and they began planning how to begin the process in Libby."

Though the Montana Study was fifty years in the past, one community member who had been part of it still lived in Libby. Inez Herrig had been chairman of the Libby study group and visited the classroom to talk with the kids. "Listen to one another and find out what you want for your community," she advised them.

High school senior Sarah Fisher said that she joined the project because she'd read the minutes of the 1947 study. "I was amazed at what they did," she said, "and I wondered if we could do it again."

Libby was facing hard times. The local economy had been built on logging, but the mills were gone, timber sales on federal lands were down, and new technologies reduced the number of jobs needed to accomplish what little logging still went on. As with most towns facing economic devastation, Libby had plenty of angry, depressed, and frightened people with lots of blame for how things had happened. A sociological study of the town commissioned by the U.S. Forest Service had found that, after a breakdown in a formal process set up to create an environmental and economic plan through community forums, it had become dangerous to talk about politics in Libby. Passions ran so high that even calling a public meeting seemed risky.

A local pastor observed that after its economic devastation, the community went through the stages of grieving, from denial, to anger, to negotiation. And now, led by invitations from its young people, it seemed ready to think about getting on with the adventure of living.

Amid this recent history, grownups and kids together set about researching and talking over the real problems they faced, including the economic future of their town and how it fit into state, national, and global trends. The goal was not to solve the problems so much as to investigate them—to look at them from various angles to see what might be seen. Each meeting combined historical reports—coresearched by adults and students on such topics as the history of the logging mills in the area and the town's relationship to the timber industry—with discussions about the town's past, its present, and its future.

Jeff Gruber's humility—he didn't pretend to be an expert on the topics the group took up—proved to be a powerful leadership style. He was curious and interested in what others could teach him. At the first meeting he was very nervous. People were sizing each other up, wondering what the real agenda might be, and asking questions he couldn't answer about where things were headed. "I found myself wondering what I was getting myself, my students, and my town into. If this was democracy, I didn't like it," he said.

"But before the meeting was completed, we had learned our first of many valuable lessons, that out of conflict comes growth. People were encouraged by their youth reaching out to them and saying 'let's have a fresh look at Libby.'"

Paul Rumelhart had a degree in philosophy but for years he hadn't had much occasion to use that education. He'd been busy with his retail petroleum business, and after some bad political experiences centered on the school, he had quit paying attention to public life in general and the schools in particular. "This was an amazing experience," he said of the new Montana Study. "I learned a lot about Libby and its history, but it wasn't what we learned that was most important. It was the attitude that developed."

When the study was finished, he stayed involved in his town's civic life. Like many veterans of political wrangling, he had learned to sidestep the distrust and anger we encounter when we try to change things. Politics at its best is teaching, which means the leader tries to stay in the "zone of proximal development," where people are challenged but not overwhelmed. He smiled quickly when problems were pointed out to him, and looked for the next step.

There were historical opponents in the room, but since the process aimed at understanding the complexities of the situation they faced, they concentrated on explaining, providing history, and putting the evidence for their thinking on the table. And since they had come to the meeting specifically to help young people understand, they avoided fights. Young people bring out the best in us.

"The hardest part was patience," said Paul. "We're so used to looking for immediate results that it's hard to take time to let the process work. And though we did hours of research and learned a lot of things along the way, more important than specific facts was that as we began to trust each other more, we began to speak more simply, more clearly and more honestly. We began to ask for clarification, to help each other use words more carefully.

"Along with our young people, we gained confidence in our ability to understand each other and the problems that we faced." But, he stressed, "It takes time. The most difficult hurdle is to get over wanting immediate results."

"Friendships were formed and old relationships were renewed," Jeff said. "We talked about what kind of people we have been. We noted that we were not very open to outsiders, and never have been. We ran Chinese people out of the gold camps in 1890. When Kootenai Dam was created, we talked about 'the dam people' who came during the construction boom it triggered in the late 1960s and early 1970s. We never looked upon them as members of our community. Now the new immigrants are retired people and locals were feeling jealousy because of their money and security."

One member, a county commissioner, said, "I've been here for 28 years but I've learned quite a bit from this. It's opened my eyes to a lot of different reasons things have happened and what has been done in the past. It's almost like a circle and things are coming around again."

The group developed an "insight statement" that summarized the attitude that had developed: "If we lose faith in each other and in our institutions, we become a collection of individuals surviving in the same space, but if we grow in our faith in each other and in our institutions, we become a community of people thriving in the same place."

Senior Mark Harmon commented that he learned, "not just about government, but also about the principles of founding a community." Sarah Fisher agreed. "This wasn't just about education," she said. "It was about civic duties and dealing with people."

At times during the discussion, grizzled veterans pondered hard questions about their community's destiny while young high school students with their gleaming skin and bright eyes stood at the white marker boards, facilitating the discussion. Outside, the cold Montana winter covered the forests with snow. Inside, people warmed to one another. A lifelong resident said at the end of the ten weeks, "this is the first time young people have gotten involved with the old goats like me."

Five years after the project, a group that had decided to stay together after the study—chaired by Paul Rumelhart—had raised enough money to begin construction of a multimillion-dollar performing arts center, to be built in the remodeled Memorial Gymnasium, a remaining tangible outcome of the first Montana Study.

Today, the 2.1-million-dollar Libby Memorial Center seems not a bad outcome for a high school civics class. The patience that Paul talked about, far from being inaction or passivity as people usually think about that virtue, turned out to be a way of acting on a larger stage, where enough time is a crucial ingredient. "There is a strict correlation between the decline of patience and the loss of the capacity for action," philosophy professor David Bailey Harned (1997) says. "They flourish together and they wither in isolation." Without patience and the long view, we lose contact with reality, flitting like excited moths around this or that bare lightbulb as though it were the sun.

People agreed that the most important "product" was the community that developed, the relationships that formed, and the spirit that they felt. The community, in other words, managed to arrest some of the processes of death that had invaded it, and began moving toward greater life. Some of the students found for the first time that scholarship has everything to do with excitement, friendship, and sharing. As most good scholars know, a special community comes into being around the pursuit of knowledge and understanding.

A few years after the Libby students did their community study, students in Renee Rasmussen's classes in Chester read what the Libby students had done and decided that if it could be done in Libby, it could be done in Chester. They invited school board members, bankers, church leaders, ranchers, and business people to meet with them in the evenings to study and discuss their community and its prospects. Brice Fenge, a high school junior, said he wanted to do the study in Chester because he wanted to make friends with older people, he wanted to learn to talk in front of a group of people, and he wanted to engage real issues in the community. Afterward, the adults who participated said they had their optimism and faith restored.

After reading the stories of what the Libby and Chester students accomplished, students in Roundup, taught by Tom Thackeray and Tim Schaff, used the model to organize their own series of community forums. They invited the community at large to a series of forums dealing with community issues such as agriculture, religion, and medicine. Their invitations led to participation by a state senator, the mayor, the director of public works, the president of the chamber of commerce, bankers, doctors, businessmen, and religious leaders. "Adaptation and searching within the community are essential to our survival," said student Lindsey Appell. The six-week program went beyond the education in most classes, said student Abby Newell. "The purpose of the study was to remind ourselves that hope is still alive if we are willing to step up to the plate."

We learn hope from stories of what others have done. The stories can be more durable and sometimes even more useful than bricks and mortar. Young people who study their communities side by side with the leaders of those communities come away with a vigorous insight into what it means to be a scholar. Such projects provide good opportunities to remind them that a single scholar can change the course of human history, and that a great community of scholars is certain to do so. Until every town and city is also, in its own way, a community of scholars, we are not making the most of the great gifts the past has prepared for us.

CHAPTER 7

Virtues and Community Character

Let us answer this book of ink with a book of flesh and blood.

—Ralph Waldo Emerson

Following Alasdair MacIntyre's (1981) enormously influential work, *After Virtue*, even quite young students can make a lot of progress toward understanding community by asking what virtues various communities practiced, and how those practices contributed to the sort of places the communities became. The study of community provides a powerful way to discuss values and moral beliefs in an objective way. We can ask what consequences have followed from various beliefs and practices, looking for examples and evidence in history—including local and family history.

The past is a vast treasury of successes and failures that formed particular kinds of communities. Lycurgus, the legendary lawgiver of ancient Sparta, supposedly believed that the virtue of egalitarianism would be important to Sparta's survival. The love of riches was a powerful threat. So he attempted to thwart avarice by using iron for money, so that handling great wealth would be inconvenient and burdensome. Alas, this turned out to be a weak barrier to such a powerful human drive. A few families managed to get control of most of the land, and most Spartans became poor. His fears were realized as society was torn apart in struggles for access to wealth.

Other parts of his program were more successful. The educational program, aimed at making the Spartans militarily formidable by emphasizing such virtues as strength, endurance, and obedience, led to a

Spartan community that not only held its own but prevailed in a tough world. The city became so confident that the Spartans lived without city walls for defense. No long security lines for them.

Sparta took its character from the virtues it chose and those virtues can be seen most vividly in the education it designed for its youth. Sparta chose the ideal of the soldier, and the rest followed. Newborns were brought before the elders and inspected for defects, to see if they would be kept. At age seven, boys were removed from their families and taken to state boarding schools, where they were trained in the gymnasium. Older boys supervised packs of younger boys, and they were given little food or bedding, so they had to become tough and re-sourceful. They were not punished for stealing food but for getting caught.

By contrast, the Roman Empire chose the ideal of the orator. This made some sense during the republican period when public speaking influenced policy, but as governing was done more and more by decree, the education for oratory became more and more ornamental. This led to what Hugh Nibley (1991) calls the rise of rhetoric and the decline of everything else. The art of rhetoric was understood as the art of per-suading the many. Like many of their cultural attainments, the Romans adopted the art of rhetoric from the Greeks. Gorgias had been its most successful promoter. He convinced himself that nothing exists, and that even if it did, we couldn't know it, and that even if we did, we couldn't communicate it. Thus liberated from the search for truth, he got on with the business of success.

Roman parents wanted the best education for their children, which was understood to be training as a rhetorician. The rhetorician was a combination lawyer, public relations specialist, politician, self-promoter, deal maker, general hustler, and entertainer in a society with-out movies or television. As education became more and more strongly associated with success, the content of that education had more and more to do with appearances and impressions. In contrast with their sturdy ancestors, the Romans cultivated the virtues of poise, wit, ele-gance, and, most of all success—defined as fame, money, and power. This led them to turn away from astronomy, music, engineering, and mathematics. When the goal of education is worldly success, those sub-jects that don't lead directly to it seem to be frills.

The empire fell apart when nobody could make sensible decisions or do anything right, and as the empire became more troubled, the public language became more lofty, magnificent, moving, and disconnected from reality. Trouble was met by speech making and posturing rather than by solutions and action.

Of course, the study of communities and the ways various virtues create characteristic places is as important for adults as it is for students. A community cannot practically discuss the educational goals it has for its children without talking about the virtues it wants to teach. This is part of the reason a focus on community is so powerful for schools—the adults and the students end up taking seriously the same questions.

There are many possibilities beyond warriors and orators. People who are attracted to heritage projects are frequently committed to making their community a place for scholarship and evidence-based thinking, respect for individual liberty and achievement, commitment to families and intergenerational learning and teaching, cooperation in communal projects, adventurousness and confidence that people can be adequate to their challenges, local self-sufficiency, and a rich diversity of people.

Virtues have gotten a lot of attention among educators of late. According to Harvard law professor Mary Ann Glendon (1995), the generation that is now running things confuses "authority and authoritarianism, and is now struggling to raise its children in a society where the former is collapsing and the latter is gaining ground. To save their children they must save the culture. That will require these busy people to find time for intelligent and vigorous involvement in the activities and institutions through which we order our lives together."

Early in my career an unfortunate cliché among educators was that "we can't teach the kids our values." But the recent outbreaks of school violence and other forms of social pathology have triggered quite a lot of talk about teaching values. Few people today think that good values don't matter or that young people will learn them if they aren't taught. Unfortunately, when such talk has led to action, it has most often been to add a program or class on ethics. While the study of ethics as an academic discipline is a worthy and fascinating endeavor, as a method of teaching young people good conduct, it lacks much force. A community's values are too deeply imbedded in a thousand realities of daily life to be greatly influenced by a special class, unless its teaching is aligned with the real-life practices of the school. Ethics are taught not primarily through ethics classes but through what teaching methods are used, how the school is governed, and how discipline is administered. The ethics that are enacted in our practices are those that we teach most powerfully.

It is quite interesting to talk with teachers, parents, and school board members about how, for example, what we teach about justice and freedom and governance in the civics curriculum coheres with what we teach about these things through the discipline code—in other words, how what Chris Argyris and Donald Schön (1974) call our "espoused theory" squares with our "theory-in-practice." Or how what we teach about compassion and courage or other virtues in the literature curriculum is illuminated by the way we interact in the hallways or during political controversies. Or how what we teach in science about analyzing data and following evidence is applied as we make the decisions that form our communal life at school. Of course, to work toward such alignment where the values schools teach and the values they practice cohere, schools and communities need to be places where the work is mindful. The basis of order at school is the mindful work of making and keeping classroom instruction of a piece with our living.

Human social systems tend toward uniformity with one set of principles governing. This was what Lincoln was getting at when he observed that a house divided against itself could not stand. He understood that slavery would either be removed completely from the Union, or in time it would spread to every state in the Union. School boards that want students treated according to one set of principles, but treat teachers according to a different set of principles, are engaged in a quite common form of folly.

Our teaching and living tend to be of a piece, though not always in ways we intend. One year student midterm reports were due in my office on a Wednesday. On Friday I went looking for a teacher who had still not turned his in. I found him in the teachers' lounge working on them. He was reviewing student work and grumbling about "kids these days." Without conscious irony that I could detect, he bellyached about "late work, missing work, incomplete work." What would it take to get kids to take assignments seriously and to turn them in on time? he wondered out loud.

What indeed? The ways human orders tend toward self-similarity, so that we see the same patterns at every level, was referred to by Jesus when he cautioned that we will be judged by the same judgment we use. More colloquially, we say that "what goes around comes around."

Anyone who spends much time in schools will see and hear things that bring home the distance we have to go if schools are to be mindful places. At a high school I visited earlier this year, some students with pacifist longings mildly protested the warrior tone of a pep assembly by sitting rather than standing during the school song. The principal was enraged at the lack of "school spirit," and on the spot he banned the group of sitting students from all school activities for the rest of the year. An indignant young scholar stood up and told him she had First Amendment rights to freedom of expression. "You weren't even saying anything," the principal shot back.

The more we try to establish order—which is not at all the same thing as organization, as can be glimpsed in the simple fact that our schools now exist at unprecedented levels of organization at the same time they exist at unprecedented levels of chaos—the more we feel prompted to remind each other to handle student rebellions, negotiate controversies at staff meetings, and treat adversaries in ways that we would be comfortable having students examine in our classrooms as examples of the sort of character we say we want. It's hard to think clearly about establishing order, in large part because we are so over-whelmed in managing our complicated organizations. This is itself a powerful teaching.

The centralizing tendencies of our state and national school systems generate tremendous noise at the local level, overwhelming conversations about what we ought to do. Instead, more and more often we need to look up what we "should" do in the various incoherent mandates, grant guidelines, accreditation reports, state office regulations, and district office memos that displace reflection and decision. People who do not feel that their destiny is in their hands find it hard to talk as if it matters about what kind of people they want to become.

So we sometimes model the virtues of busy bureaucrats: superficial intelligence, resigned flexibility, impersonal pleasantness, lackadaisical diligence, selective inattention—and we relegate talk of higher character to special classes. But Anne C. Lewis (1998) suggests that "in treating character as a separate subject rather than as a value that underlies everything, many schools have lost sight of their institutional role . . . Students need to see character demonstrated all around them, not merely to find it on a list of electives." That is, it needs to determine the very structure and function of community. "Character outside of a lived community, the entanglements of complex social relationships and their shared story is impossible," says sociology professor James Davison Hunter (2000). It is as members of groups trying to "enact a moral vision" that persons find themselves within a story that frees their aspirations and longings from the cramped quarters of individual appetites and anxieties. He points out that we save children, in large part, by telling them what we are saving them for.

To be sure, schools are not the only or even the most powerful educator of many of today's youth. That distinction belongs to the storytellers—families and churches and synagogues and mosques for lucky kids and movies and music videos and peer gangs for others. Many of the schools we have built are huge institutions many miles distant from the families they serve. Parents often leave for work before daylight and return in the evening dark, their lives disconnected from the school lives of their children.

And yet who, working in these schools, cannot feel that the school system nationwide is poised for change? This is why it seems so chaotic. What we need now are working alternatives that people can see and understand, and the important work before us now is not trying to change the larger system so much as to find new ways of working in spite of it.

Many communities are creating such alternatives. Rural communities, in particular, have been bold and innovative in finding new ways to approach schooling. In many ways, this is unsurprising. Wendell Berry (1990), musing about these things a few years ago, said, "my feeling is that if improvement is going to begin anywhere, it will have to begin out in the country and in the country towns. This is not because of any intrinsic virtue that can be ascribed to rural people, but because of their circumstances. . . . They have much reason, by now, to know how little real help is to be expected from somewhere else. They still have, moreover, the remnant of local memory and local community. And in rural communities there are still farms and small businesses that can be changed according to the will and desire of individual people."

Paul Theobold reached similar conclusions through his work in South Dakota. He examined what we need to do to redesign schools with the goal of re-creating their communities. An important key, he says, is that "the curriculum must grow out of real issues important to the students and the people in a particular community. Activities that connect with one's own experience, that require the use of skills from various disciplines, that are carried out in cooperation with others, and that result in a useful product give students the most powerful kinds of learning experiences."

The importance of individual action particularly stands out, since, as Clifford Lord (1964) points out, "change is the work of individuals." This is vivid at the local level. "The study of community history," he says, "emphasizes the continuing importance of the individual. This . . . is an important lesson to absorb early in life. The lack of an attractive foreseeable future, the sense of helplessness and hopelessness which seemingly afflicts so many of our teen-agers today, assumes its true perspective when confronted with the facts of what has happened and what is happening, who made it happen and who is making it happen in the average community today."

He concludes that it's impossible to study the history of a community—or a corporation or a college or a church—and forget for a moment that people make its history. This gives concrete, tangible, specific meaning to the continuing importance of the individual.

It seems that everyone now talks about the importance of community, probably because we sense its loss. But teachers doing heritage projects take community seriously by making both the theory and practice of community the subject of serious study. In a real sense, we improve education by improving our conversation. If we talk about standards, let's talk about what we want from them. We want clear and accurate writing that tells vivid truths about who we have been and who we are. If we talk about discipline, let's talk about how we shape the places we live by how we conduct ourselves, and so let's talk about the sort of places we want to live. Let's examine the choices that are open to people and follow the consequences of some of those choices through history. If we talk about the importance of work, let's ask various people in town how they understand work—work as career, work as jobs, work as profession, work as calling, work as drudgery, work as passion. Let's inquire into how the sexes see work differently and how they see it the same. Let's trace how work affects family. Let's see what we can find out about how different occupations develop different cultures.

The more we link our curriculum with the actual community in which we live, the more mindful we become, both in our living and in our teaching and learning. We learn to appreciate how much everything depends on individual action. We learn how much individuals owe to families and communities. We prize the continuity that keeps life predictable and explicable. We welcome the innovation that individuals and communities need to keep thriving. We learn how inexhaustibly rich are the experiences of the past, and how all innovation is fed by the past.

We see that education is inseparable from generational succession, and that the young get what they most need from their elders at the same time that elders cannot fulfill themselves except through investing in youth. We value taking care of things that have to last. We plan how to restore what we learn we should have taken care of. As poet Theodore Roethke put it, we learn by going where we have to go. We find as Robert Frost found that what we will not part with we are unaccountably allowed to keep.

I imagine that when new community histories are written fifty years from now, the heritage projects begun by many teachers, students, and community members today will have grown into marvelous works that we can at present scarcely imagine, and that those who began these projects will be rightly understood by those future researchers to be among the community's most significant pioneers and leaders.

Eight Practices of Community-Centered Teachers

"Ah," said the mouse, "the world is growing narrower every day. At first it was so wide that I felt anxious. I kept running and was happy to see finally walls to the right and left of me in the distance, but these walls are speeding so fast toward each other that I am already in the last room and there in the corner stands the trap into which I'm running."

"You need only change the direction in which you're running," said the cat and gobbled it up.

—Kafka

Teachers in the Montana Heritage Project developed a set of eight core practices. They represent hours of conversations among skilled teachers working in several academic disciplines (though predominantly English and history) over several years with hundreds of students.

1. Teachers use the community as the subject of serious study. The dual emphasis on community and study is important. There are lots of ways to celebrate community that don't necessarily lead to stronger scholarship. A pep assembly is one example.

But to make community a central topic of study is to say that community is important, worthy of our best efforts to understand. A huge educational advantage to studying local communities is that they are available for study. We cannot understand the world except by understanding particular places. Federalism may begin to make sense to a student who has seen the way the local town council interacts with state and federal mandates by doing a case study of how a local issue unfolds.

Through studying the history of a community that existed before they arrived and will continue to exist after they leave, young people move toward understanding the complex relationships between place and time and a people. They develop a personal connection to history and to place.

Theresa Marche (1998) suggests three roles students may take in studying their communities.

First, they may become hunter-gatherers, collecting artifacts and materials from the community environment. Students operate somewhat like shoppers, seeking "interesting objects, stories, and experiences" outside the classroom.

Second, students may approach their communities as "detectives," asking such questions as "What is this community about and how did it get this way?" Students research the "historical origins and present configurations of their local community, its arts, occupations, and celebrations."

And third, students may see themselves as participants, asking how they might act upon the world outside the classroom. They study "architecture, land use, social/cultural interactions, and a wide range of environmental sciences" while being encouraged to "develop a sense of place and stewardship for that place."

The focus on community transforms many community members into experts—business people, local historians, old-timers in rest homes, artists, forest managers, farmers, loggers, politicians—all are expert on some aspect of community life. In a similar spirit, each student should be assisted and encouraged to become the world's leading authority on something. This isn't as intimidating as it sounds. I sat in on an interview student Karista James from Corvallis was conducting with an eighty-year-old man, Junior, who had spent his early years in the abandoned gold mining town of Rochester that she was researching. Karista was a beautiful girl with large brown eyes and long dark hair. Junior wore a blue cowboy shirt with a contrasting yoke, his white hair tousled in a Will Rogers cut.

Junior's house in Twin Bridges, a few miles from Rochester, was filled with boxes and albums of old photographs of the area. He had been spending hours putting them in order, and was delighted to have an audience that was interested in what he knew. Karista had read everything that had been published about Rochester, which wasn't a terrific amount. She had also spent time in the Montana Historical Society archives. She was part of a team of students who were assisting the Bureau of Land Management in doing a field archaeology project at the site. Karista had spent hours trying to put together Rochester's stories in her head. At one point, Junior mentioned a fire that burned out part of the business district in Rochester. "After that, nothing was the same," he said.

Karista interrupted him, intent on what he was saying. "Do you mean the Hardesty Hotel fire?" she asked.

Junior paused and looked at her in a new way. He was an old man, living alone with old photographs and old memories. Who really cared about all that? Well, Karista cared. Knowledge takes time and work, and she cared enough to know.

One of the interesting things that became clear as I traveled to other interviews with Karista and the other students on her research team was that they knew more about Rochester than any of their interview subjects. They had pursued leads and possibilities through the archives, and had been able to identify two people buried in graves in the cemetery under headstones that said simply "unknown." They had spent weekends wandering the site, collecting and cataloging all the objects within staked out areas, analyzing the economic classes of various neighborhoods by the quality of the foundations left where no buildings remained. They had collected dozens of old photographs showing the town at various stages in its history, and they had interviewed anyone who might be able to shed light on the town's past.

One of the mysteries of Rochester referred to in the published materials was that nobody knew where its name had come from. Interviewing an old farmer in Twin Bridges, the students asked to see the nineteenth-century deed to the original home sites at Rochester purchased by his grandfather. They learned that he had purchased his land from a man named Rochester.

Without a doubt, the kids in Corvallis were the world's leading authorities on the history of Rochester, and they knew it. This is powerfully motivational. Such opportunities lie everywhere around us. Students can become experts on the histories of specific buildings, city parks, community organizations and agencies, clubs, businesses, and occupations and crafts. They can gather unpublished information about how national events, such as World War II or the coming of the automobile affected the local community. They can write the unwritten stories of their own ancestors' lives.

By going into the community as journalists, historians, documentarians, artists, scientists—and as members—young people practice listening, speaking, collaborating, presenting evidence, and collecting and organizing information. Their education is brought to life.

One danger of local studies is that local historians can take too provincial a view of affairs. It's important not to fall into the error of teaching that the local place is better than other places. Instead, the emphasis should be on how we understand any place by studying its history, nature, and folklife. Having learned to understand and care for one place, students are better prepared to understand and care for other places. It is important to study local history as a part of national and world history with a broadening education as the goal.

This isn't hard to do. Renee Rasmussen's classes in Chester began examining an abandoned house made of large bricks manufactured at the home site. No one had lived there since before World War I. The students carefully documented the house, with photographs, maps, floor plans, and descriptions of the architectural detail. But they also dug into the historical record at the county courthouse to find out who had owned the land, where the owner came from, and where the owner went. It became a fascinating story.

In brief, the house was built by Estonians, who had fled Russia because of the Bolshevik Revolution. The Enlarged Homestead Act had drawn them to Montana. After two good years, a devastating drought caused them to leave. Most of the students, before they began studying the building, knew nothing about the revolution in Russia, the promotional schemes of railroads to lure people to land too dry to farm, or the drought that brought so much heartbreak to homesteaders throughout Montana.

By the end of their project, the students knew quite a lot about all these things, and they told the story in words, newspaper clippings, oral interviews with third generation Estonians, and photographs that would become a permanent part of their community's memory. They saw how a small town on the Great Plains fit into the grand narrative of world history, and they felt a personal connection to events far away in time and space. They made the story accessible to others in the community and to researchers in the future. They had learned but they had also contributed to a legacy.

Taking community seriously makes good pedagogical sense for other reasons, too. Many adolescents have not yet developed adult capacities for abstract, formal thought, and it's easy for teachers to talk in ways that make virtually no sense to them, given their limited experience of the world and their fledgling powers of abstract conceptualization. In the community, concepts in history, literature, and science can be explored. Local politics, for example, has all the patterns that are seen in national politics—factions, nobility, rumors, power plays, deception, idealism, and cynicism. Seeing the dynamics up close in concrete, known situations gives young people the experiential base needed to make sense of larger-scale and more distant processes.

The study of community also supports the most important developmental learning that occurs during the teenage years. According to Harvard psychologist Robert Kegan (1994), the greatest educational need of young people from about age twelve to age twenty or so is in nothing other than learning about community. Adolescents are at the developmental stage where they are just beginning to form and join communities.

He points out that teachers, parents, employers, coaches, church leaders, policemen, neighbors, and civic leaders all want, more than anything, for teenagers to develop the level of consciousness we refer to as "being a good citizen." The entire community needs—in some cases desperately—its young people to develop an understanding of and a loyalty to various communities, stepping beyond their immediate personal desires. They need to become better at being members of teams and families. They need to understand the reasons for rules and to share those reasons, moving from childlike obedience to a more mature taking of responsibility.

Kegan suggests that "an integrating vision" for American schooling "may be found in an unrecognized curriculum: the culture's widespread demand for a common transformation of mind during adolescence." That common transformation amounts to this: that students learn to see their families, teams, classrooms, and neighborhoods not just as an environment in which they pursue their individual desires, but as communities in which they are members. All the families and communities that form the larger town and city communities share an urgent desire for teenagers to join decent, wholesome communities. Teaching them how to do this and what it might mean should be a central organizing principle of the high school years.

Such an integrating vision is badly needed in other ways as well. Most school reformers today recognize that fragmentation—of the curriculum, of the school day, of the school's mission—is a serious obstacle to sensible schooling. It is not a minor consideration that "community study is naturally integrative . . . [It] invites the young to focus naturally on realities, avoiding curricular segmentation that is often meaningless" (Beery and Schug, 1984).

Without some such integration, Thomas Sergiovanni (1994) suggests that schools will have difficulty meeting their scholarly missions. The goal is for "schools to become places where relationships are family-like, where space and time resemble a neighborhood, and where a code of values and ideas is shared."

2. Teachers look for chances for students to do real work. The best projects grow out of authentic local needs and the desires of people to have the communities they really want. The students in Broadus teamed up with the Powder River County Historical Museum to create audio walking tours of the exhibits. The museum was already organized into stations, such as "Women and Rodeo" and "saddles." By doing research in published books and courthouse records and by conducting oral interviews, students were able to write and record scripts that provided museum visitors with a richer experience than the interpretive signs in the museum.

Students in Libby began organizing, cataloguing, and filing historical photographs for the local museum. Soon, they were collecting photographs from the entire community. As word of their project spread, people brought them historical photographs to be duplicated and preserved. Students began spending more time at the museum, getting involved in more aspects of its work. This led to the school administration approving a special class that meets at the museum rather than at the school so students could work in an apprenticeship relationship with heritage professionals.

Another team of Libby students created a brochure during the last year of operation of the local lumber mill. They documented in words and photos each of the processes that went on in the mill that had provided the economic underpinnings to their community for generations before it was shut down forever.

The community of Howard, South Dakota, experienced economic hardship following the farm crisis of the 1980s. Paul Theobald and Jim Curtiss (2000) write that "in 1994, a new principal . . . asked his high school staff a question that is scarcely ever asked by school leaders: what can we do in the school to help this community?" In response, the business teacher invited students "to study the community's cash flow—how much was earned there, where it was spent, and what it was spent for. The students conducted town meetings with local business owners, consulted with the county auditor, and engaged in long debates with all stakeholders over the wording on their surveys."

This gave the students a chance to learn and apply important academic skills. They "found themselves with a phenomenal 64 percent response rate and an enormous amount of data to analyze. Using sophisticated computer software, the students sorted the data by income level, spending location, spending category, and other parameters."

Their findings as reported in the local paper showed that "the people of Howard spent most of their income in the larger and more distant cities of Madison, Mitchell, and Sioux Falls." The response, Theobald and Curtiss report, "was a little short of amazing." Community members changed their spending habits. They began doing more of their shopping locally. "Revenue from local sales tax began to skyrocket. The county auditor reported that by the end of the summer, annual sales tax projections had already been exceeded. Based on the average number of times a locally spent dollar will turn over within a community, the county auditor estimated that the students had engineered a $6 to $7 million infusion into Howard's economy."

The students from Corvallis who did research in Rochester were helping the Bureau of Land Management. That federal agency had archaeological expertise but not sufficient staff to do a field archaeology project. Teaming up was a natural partnership. The agency provided high-quality academic instruction and training while meeting its own mission, and the school provided eager workers. Another team of

Corvallis students in a senior research class teamed up with the Montana Department of Fish, Wildlife, and Parks to collect onsite data throughout the year documenting elk and human interactions on the Calf Creek Wildlife Refuge. In exchange for their work, they received training in designing a research project and then collecting and interpreting data.

Such opportunities are limited only by the imaginations of community members, inside and outside the school. Museums, libraries, parks, wildlife refuges, as well as many government offices and businesses have research projects that it would benefit them to undertake, if they only had the staff.

At the same time many high school students are languishing away at school, not doing much of anything. In *The Unschooled Mind*, Howard Gardner (1991) urges educators to reconsider the value of that ancient teaching model, the apprenticeship. Students who work as cognitive apprentices to knowledge workers receive the sort of teaching helpful for deep understanding, including immersion in an information-rich environment, working with others, and demonstrations of mastery.

3. Teachers encourage young people to study the lives of people who are not rich or powerful or famous. Asserting that such lives have value helps students and teachers find the basis for making their own community at school one in which all students, even the troubled ones and the poor performers, are valued. If we believe and teach that everyone is important, we make it true, and such a belief is an organizing theme of community-centered teaching.

"Every community is a monument to the men and women who made it," Clifford Lord (1964) points out. "The men who surveyed the streets and later paved them, then used them for the installation of water, sewer, and electric facilities; to the men who opened the first stores . . . to the editor who pilloried all transgression, real or imaginary, so mercilessly that for a generation he created a different climate of public morality and left behind a tradition with which others could conjure; to the minister whose evangelical zeal for the Social Gospel and for the dignity of every human being made the town a better place in which to live; to the patron whose generosity made possible special cultural opportunities in the town; to the teacher who opened new horizons to generation after generation of students."

Though celebrity still dazzles, most serious scholars have awakened to the need to study ordinary people to make sense of the world. Our desire for understanding, liberated by modern wealth and leisure, has filled us with an appetite for the details. This appetite will continue growing as new tools make searching and organizing enormous amounts of information possible. We once had more limited means and felt we could afford to save detailed information only about the kings and lords, but we now have the means to gather and save information about everyone. Astonishing advances in computerized searching are quickly making such information increasingly useable, indeed indispensable, to future scholars.

We can't even know for sure what will be of most value to researchers down the road. After a rash of book burning in the seventh century, Buddhist monks set about the work of writing their scriptures on stone tablets. The task took a thousand years. Stewart Brand (2000) notes that though the scriptures are useful "we might value the stones more if the monks had simply recorded the weather or what they were eating." Even their poop, he says, saved systematically would provide a treasure of data for research about agriculture, diet, disease, genetics, and so on. We do not need to be unusually brilliant to contribute to the great project of human knowledge.

There is not one elder in your town whose life story is not worth recording and contemplating, and we will fall short of realizing our humanity until we have made a systematic effort to do just that. If every high school senior were invited to bring to the community archives one such story every year, many of the problems we now face would begin a quiet process of healing themselves.

Those elders who have struggled profoundly with intellectual and spiritual questions and can share their insights and conclusions will do us a great favor. But every story has things to teach, and we cannot predict what will be of most value. We need to understand not just our great artists and sages, our political and military leaders, but also the poor souls such as those in the Donner party who, overcome by hunger, violated their own taboos, or the young man wrenched from his home in Africa, bound in the hold of a whaling vessel heading toward a different world in which he would no longer be viewed as human.

In a mysterious way, people in the past aren't gone. They are waiting. When we find their stories, and are changed by them, their lives
move nearer to fulfillment. If you doubt this, do research in primary
sources about a person you can find some way to admire. Try to help
her by understanding her in ways that make you rethink some aspect of
your own life. As you let her help you, you help her, and you can trust
that the feelings stirring within you are confirmation that you are on the
right path.

The past is never finished. Every year, new people find out what the
Renaissance or the American Revolution or the migration of a grandfather from Russia was all about, and as they do that, their horizons
change. And as each person changes, the world itself is changed.
Teachers who have taught today's young people by accompanying
them into the personal and tangible stories, both present and past, that
make up the communities that surround them, have seen that for many
young people, this is exactly what they need.

*4. Teachers emphasize "gifts" to the community as the final product
of their students' academic research.* Every research project is understood to be a service project: providing written biographies for the families of rest home residents, creating a written history for a community
organization, submitting a nomination to the National Register of Historic Places for a building owned by a local church, organizing a collection of research papers for the local library's archives, creating a
photo essay on a community event for the local museum, or writing
family history for one's own family.

Many young people don't resist such projects. Though many of them
have developed a sort of free-floating irreverence, such irreverence is often a defense for an underlying idealism, and many young people are
looking for someone and something to believe in. On numerous surveys
they have listed the creation of strong families as their highest priority, and
they are returning to church in greater numbers than their parents. When
they meet leaders who speak authentically, they are willing to listen. What
young people most need are older people who accept the challenge.

It's true that young people today are less interested in national politics, less trusting of government, less committed to political parties,
and more concerned about their economic futures than earlier generations. After all, they have access to the news and they aren't fools.

Some of today's youth feel that they are inheriting a world with serious economic, political, and environmental problems, but that the political parties are more interested in making each other look bad and peddling themselves to the highest bidders than they are in fixing anything. Rather than joining large organizations, today's youth prefer to put their energy into local activities where they can see real change.

At the same time, many older people feel unfulfilled by their work in large and impersonal organizations. After years of studying the problem of living with the massive organizations and rapid change of modern life, Peter Drucker (1998), one of the greatest management thinkers of the twentieth century, concludes that what we need most right now cannot be provided by either our government or our business organizations. Adults need three things that they are not finding, he says: they need communities, they need effective citizenship, and they need to volunteer. We need to feel our independence by acting outside the rule-bound institutions where many of us work, and we need to feel our lives are making a difference.

Obviously, these adult needs are congruent with what our young people are looking for. They do not need busy work that matters only because of a hypothetical future, but real and important work performed in a web of personal relationships, personal expectations, personal praise, and personal disapproval—that is, they need personal teaching, not just from one adult, but from many people in the community, including scientists, grandmothers, farmers, artists, house builders, nurses, cowboys, foresters, ministers, bankers, scholars, and politicians—anyone who is an expert on some aspect of what it takes to build and sustain a community—which is to say, everyone.

5. Teachers incorporate intergenerational research into every project. Renee Rasmussen wanted a community forum in which her high school students could read their local history research papers to the community, so elementary principal Vi Hill organized a community heritage fair. Old-time crafts such as butter churning and wood carving were demonstrated for elementary students. Vintage cars and horses and buggies were available for rides. Old-timers played their music in the lunchroom. Various groups put up displays of artifacts brought by immigrants from the old country, or did presentations on such topics as the history of medicine in the town. Classes were canceled, and more than five hundred people came to the school to celebrate their diverse heritage with one another.

One of the presentations was a fashion show. Girls modeled their grandmothers' wedding dresses, and while they walked across the stage, the narrator told the story of the wedding and the subsequent marriage. This ended up being an effective way to tell much of the community's history—one of the dresses was handmade from parachute silk because of a fabric shortage during World War II—but as always, other things were happening too.

In the telling, an important community folkway was vigorously endorsed by its oldest living exemplars: these were a people who believed in marriage. A young woman bought the most elaborate dress she would ever wear, wore it once, then put it away and saved it forever. The young people stood up in front of the entire community and made promises in public. Everyone brought them gifts.

The seventy- and eighty-year-old women were suddenly transformed, as it became easy for everyone to visualize them as they had appeared when they were married. A sense of time became tangible in the auditorium for young and old alike. Most of the couples had faced serious challenges but few seemed to feel any longer that having problems was much of a problem. Trouble was the only chance you got to show what you were made of.

Community-centered teaching is not just good for kids. It provides developmentally appropriate learning for elders as well. When the students in Red Lodge, Montana, set out to write biographies of elders who lived in the local rest home, the patient care coordinator said that this was the most important service that could be provided to many of the residents. "It's just what they need to resolve their own life issues," she said.

Old people need to reflect on their experiences just as surely as toddlers need to gather experiences. They need to come to meaning about their lives, and this is hard to do without telling their stories, and it's hard to tell the stories if no one comes to listen.

When Mary Sullivan's classes at Bigfork High School began conducting oral interviews with the residents of a nearby rest home, other family members began showing up at the interviews, bringing photographs and documents. David Scoles from Broadus finished a mural depicting the stages of his grandfather's life the day before his grand-father died. He said he wouldn't have had the interviews that went into his artwork without the school assignment. In an important sense, these students are not just recording history, they are making history. Such poignant events become a daily reality for teachers and students work-ing together to create local legacies.

Youth and maturity find what they need in each other. The pattern begins in infancy, as babies get what they need from parents while, at the same time, teaching young adults how to be parents. The pattern continues throughout life. It is in mentoring youth that maturity finds its deepest fulfillment. The desire to hold on to things and to remain in control will be frustrated, one way or another, and older people sooner or later face the inescapable choice between losing everything or pass-ing on what they can.

What they can pass on are precisely those things that hold their value, that change most slowly if they change at all. Older people are best qualified to know which things are transient and ephemeral and which are of lasting worth, and this is the knowledge that allows them to provide direction to the exuberant energies of youth.

At the same time, it is a great solace for each older person to realize that the legacy he or she has that will be of greatest worth to the future is precisely what every person values most: the story of his or her own life. Stories of what individual persons faced, what they were given, what they could not find, what they lost, what they kept, what they at-tempted, what happened, how they came to think about it, in all the specificity of the times and places they lived, become more not less valuable with the passage of time. "I weep for the questions I didn't think to ask," says writer William Kittredge, thinking of family stories now lost.

Intergenerational teaching and learning helps rebuild trust between the community and the school, and to engage parents and grandparents in the educational mission of the school. At the most pragmatic possi-ble level, several schools have reported success at passing operational levies and bond issues for new buildings after extensive oral history projects that put interested teenagers in the homes of the elderly throughout the community. Older people often feel no personal con-nection to the schools though they still vote, and bands of teenagers one doesn't know can seem a crass and frightening lot. But most are nice people, when you get to know them.

6. Teachers focus on history and folklife, helping students to see and understand change, continuity, and conflict, bringing the past to bear on contemporary problems. Many history texts subtly imply a message of historical inevitability—that things have turned out as they had to or as they were supposed to. But in history encountered through local newspaper archives and oral interviews, the freedom of characters to act and react is emphasized. The study of history makes clear that much of our destiny is in our hands.

Neil Postman (1996) argues that all subjects should be taught from a historical perspective.

Every academic discipline can be thought of as what Robert M. Hutchins called a "great conversation," but kids can't understand the conversation when they are taught that knowledge is fixed, having arrived in their textbooks by some form of immaculate conception. "To teach about the atom without including Democritus in the conversation, electricity without Faraday, political science without Aristotle or Machiavelli, astronomy without Ptolemy, is to deny our students access to the Great Conversation," Postman (1996) says. It is only by learning that knowledge has a past that students begin to see that it also has a future, and that their work is to be participants in making that future.

By emphasizing local and family history students are led to examine their own lives as members of families and participants in specific communities, and Beery and Schug (1984) suggest this adds a historical dimension to their awareness of self and develops a sense of personal connection to the community and the past.

While students are learning research, writing, and presentation skills, they are also becoming members of the community. Teacher Phil Leonardi at Corvallis High School stages a Heritage Evening each spring, in which students tell the community stories that are vital to its folklife, through videotapes that feature oral histories, historical photographs, and information gathered from archival research.

Sophomore Kate Campbell created a segment on "adversity." She had researched a fire that had destroyed the Corvallis school on January 15, 1930. "In a matter of minutes it forced two hundred grammar school students and ninety-six high school students out into the bitter snow, where fifteen below zero winds were blowing. It was one of the coldest days that winter." As two-hundred community members listened, Kate told some of their stories back to them, reminding them that they had gotten through hard times in the past by being a community rather than trying to go it alone.

On the screen, Mabel Popham, now elderly, described the fire: "I had gotten a new coat for Christmas—that was in 1929 and the beginning of the Depression—and I couldn't stop to pick up my coat. Everybody just got out. That was the main thing, to escape the fire. And everybody did get out, everyone was safe, but everybody lost their coats that they got for Christmas, which was kind of traumatic at that time because it was the beginning of the Depression."

Kate studied how the community responded. "Buildings such as the Masonic Temple, a school in a neighboring town, and various churches were offered to house school children in need of a warm place to learn. Many people freely gave time, talents and money to help out wherever and whenever they were needed. The network of support that developed because of a community disaster became vital as the Depression worsened."

A few months after that Heritage Evening, Corvallis's middle school caught fire and was destroyed. People seemed to know instantly how they should react. Their own lore, taught to them by one of their children who had learned it from one of their elders, served as a guide.

Altruism, compassion, honesty, and peacefulness can be taught as surely as phonics and math, though they aren't taught in ethics classes so much as by communities enacting themselves. Folklife is more fundamentally educative than rationalized curricula. By sending youth into their communities to discover how current institutions came into being and how they have adjusted to events over time, what obstacles the older generation faced and how they acted and what happened as a result—in brief, by focusing on what sort of people they were and what happened to them—Phil Leonardi was bringing his students home to a civilizing community. The lines blur between telling the stories and living them.

7. Teachers insist upon education and scholarship as the primary focus of schooling. Scholars have developed their own virtues that include honesty, a commitment to forming questions in ways that they can be answered by research, respect for evidence and the rules of evidence developed by the various academic disciplines, a readiness to examine situations from various perspectives, and to withhold judgment while developing understanding.

Every student can contribute something of permanent worth to the record, and the classroom is organized to help students make those contributions. For the students' work to be fully realized, the community needs a permanent archive. Arrangements can be made with a local museum or historical society to collect and preserve the work students have done, or an archive can be created in the school library. For a time, a file cabinet in a classroom could suffice. The important thing is that high-quality work is kept with the intention of permanent preservation, and that students know this is the goal. Before they were transferred from the high school history classroom to the community's Heritage Museum, the historical photo archives collected by students at Libby High School were used for research by students at the local college.

It can be hard, at the beginning, for people to see the value of such collections. We are accustomed to schoolwork being done in a play world apart from the real world. Our classrooms try to simulate the real world to give the work the appearance of meaning, as when teachers begin assignments with such guidelines as "imagine you are planning a museum exhibit" or "pretend you are the owner of small business" and other ways of trying to connect schoolwork to real world concerns. But a general rule of thumb might be that whenever schoolwork can be done in the real world, it should be. Students can work with museum professionals to design real exhibits. Students can operate real businesses from school.

When the collection is small—a handful of essays and photographs—it isn't a powerful resource. Such things take time. But we have time. Fifty years from now, people will still be here. Wouldn't it be wonderful if students fifty years from now could begin their senior research projects by browsing the digital archives, looking at the hundreds of research projects on the local community that are there, examining some of the thousands of historical photographs that were preserved and labeled?

Perhaps a girl would look through an environmental history of her home valley done by students twenty years before, and become intrigued by mention of the ways Native Americans had once burned the underbrush in the forests to make pasture available. Maybe she would have an idea for how to provide a more detailed chapter on that portion of the record.

Or maybe a boy would read an essay on the homestead era, and how people came to his hometown on the Great Plains because of free land and trouble at home between the Bolsheviks and Estonians. Maybe he would recall that his ancestors came from Estonia, prompting him to add to the archives the story of one ancestor, and what he faced, and what he recorded in diaries that are still tucked away with old pictures in the family album.

Maybe a team of students would find a forty-year-old study of frog populations done on a local stream, and redo the study, comparing current data with the historical record. Maybe a different team would find a set of twenty photographs made at a recorded date from recorded vantage points, and decide to take a new set of photographs from the same locations, to examine changing vegetation patterns.

The nature of research is that the more of it that is done the more we see to do. If you visualize our body of knowledge as a sphere, then as we increase the size of that sphere, its edge, which is where our ignorance begins, also increases. The more we learn, the more we don't know and the more questions we have.

Most of the best ideas will come from teachers as the project of creating legacies of local research moves forward. Most of our historical legacy does not exist in museums. Most of it exists in family records, boxes of heirlooms, prized letters and diaries, and family photo albums. Most streams and meadows and forests have not been the subject of even basic research. Historian Elliott West believes that this vast body of uncollected and uncataloged information is the real frontier of historical research.

As we help our students move toward being creators of their own sense of place, they begin to awaken to the world around them. They begin to educate themselves.

8. Teachers appreciate and use the educational power of narratives. Because adolescents are engaged in forming identities which have a narrative structure, and they model their very selves on stories they get from the narrative environment, educators cannot ignore that environment. Though the current emphasis in education, driven by mandated accountability programs that rely on testing regimes, is upon learning at lower levels than that of narrative, forces will conspire to ensure that schools in the near future cannot ignore the narrative environment. It is becoming increasingly clear that young people caught up in bad stories are a menace to themselves and others, and that the only antidote to a bad story is a better story. The competition between stories will increase. The best story will win.

More and more people are coming to understand again that communities, education, and stories are inextricably bound together. Yale anthropologist Keith H. Basso (1986) quotes Nick Thompson, an Apache elder, who explains something of the way stories operate in his community:

> This is what we know about our stories. They go to work on your mind and make you think about your life. Maybe you've not been acting right. Maybe you've been stingy. Maybe you've been chasing after women. Maybe you've been trying to act like a Whiteman. People don't like it! So someone goes hunting for you—maybe your grandmother, your grandfather, your uncle. It doesn't matter. Anyone can do it.
>
> So someone stalks you and tells a story about what happened long ago. It doesn't matter if other people are around—you're going to know he's aiming that story at you. All of a sudden it hits you! It's like an arrow, they say . . . Then you feel weak, real weak, like you are sick. You don't want to eat or talk to anyone. That story is working on you now. You keep thinking about it. That story is changing now, making you want to live right. That story is making you want to replace yourself.
>
> It's hard to keep living right. Many things jump up at you and block your way. But you won't forget that story.

Of course, it isn't just Apaches who surround their young with webs of stories. All cultures do the same thing. Teachers engaged in community-centered teaching try to surround young people with stories drawn from the places they live that teach them powerful, compassionate, intelligent, and moral ways to live. These stories create a narrative environment in which all students understand that by helping with heritage projects they become scholars, creating gifts that the community needs and wants. They remind young people along the way that their heritage includes the great conversation of all cultures and all academic disciplines of which the local community is a part. To possess this heritage, they need to join the conversation, which means not just listening but also contributing. That's real work. They contribute by working with others to complete heritage projects, which start with what is known and move toward what is unknown, gradually converting ignorance to knowledge.

We are at a moment in history when we have the experience, the tools, and the wealth to consider anew what it all means. Computers have given researchers in many disciplines new tools—DNA sampling, the interpretation of ancient manuscripts, noninvasive archaeological analysis of aerial photographs—to pose and answer questions about the past that few people imagined only years ago. The bright side of the heritage crusades forming around the planet today is that more and more people are drawn to study the past, looking for meaning. In America, family history research, which is real research, has become more popular than any pastime except gardening.

The past is our future. We can no more stop the huge project of re-creating the past to understand it better than we could have stopped the Industrial Revolution. Our tremendous opportunities outweigh our terrifying problems, by a little.

If our communities seem troubled, or if our schools have lost direction, or if students seem lost, we need to evaluate the narrative environment with an eye to revision.

CHAPTER 9

It's about Time

Education is the point at which we decide whether we love the world enough to assume responsibility for it.

—Hannah Arendt, *Teaching as Leading*

John Dewey's ideal high school was to be built around two large central rooms. The first was a library. That part of the vision we've mostly realized. The second, though, was a museum. That part of the vision we're just beginning to understand. Howard Gardner (1991) recently wondered what would happen if instead of enrolling students in school at age six, we enrolled them in museums. Not a museum where docents give guided tours and offer preformulated scraps of learning, and not a museum designed as a tourist attraction, but a museum as a place where the local world is studied and interpreted, a museum as a work center where young and old together decide what needs to be remembered, what needs to be learned, and what stories need to be told.

We wouldn't want to have the museum without accompanying archives. Archives remind us that time is vast and reliable. It doesn't run out. It's inexhaustible.

TIME, CHANGE, AND THE INVISIBLE WORLD

Every good craftsman, whether working in wood or in words or in other symbols, learns eventually that to do a good job, it's important to believe that time is sufficient. Hurrying would be a mistake. The hasty

man, the Chinese proverb tells us, eats soup with a fork. All the difficulties we face can be solved if we think in the necessary time frames.
Some problems require years of work. Some require decades, and some
require generations. Artists experience time as the ground from which
their sensibility bodies forth into the world. For them as for lovers, time
is deep and endless. There is enough and more.

Time is the very stuff of life. What we make of it is ultimately all we
are. Introducing young people to the depths of time and what has happened there is important work. We should introduce them to the sense
of time as an inexhaustible wealth. It's our primary resource in becoming ourselves.

Unfortunately, it's easy to experience time in school in somewhat the
way it's experienced by prisoners and slaves: as a burden. When students can do no real work, but only tasks and chores, their identity becomes weak and faint. Hope fades. Time hangs. The clock barely
moves. Desire asphyxiates.

Researchers who have gone into classrooms to study what happens
there report that much of the time little happens. Things are controlled
but not much occurs. People goof off, but not with much zest, and nobody really cares. Boredom and lethargy rule. When we pass through
airports, we are reminded of the way the administered life drifts toward
endless lines, endless forms, slow motion organization and the pervasive feeling of impotence to accelerate or change what happens. Time,
the very stuff of life, is wasted.

We get nothing done by dissipating ourselves in a thousand tasks.
This is the plight not just of students but of many of us today. The modern world took form with and through technologies for organizing time.
In the early 1400s a new technology—clocks—changed people's relationship to each other by increasing their ability to coordinate their activities. The first clocks were much too large and expensive for individual ownership, so huge clock towers were built in the centers of
many towns. The periodic tolling of great iron bells drifted through the
countryside. Folks were suddenly able to coordinate individual schedules with new precision. They found themselves collaborating—not always by choice—in ways they had not previously imagined.

Today, we live in an extraordinarily organized society in which all of
us keep, or are kept by, schedules. Our highly elaborated and precise

sense of time has allowed for a society organized to an unprecedented degree, within which nearly all of us are specialists. An artist ordering invitations for a show featuring his old-fashioned oil paintings might drop his sketch off at a quick print franchise on Main Street. He need not be at all aware of what happens next: with clocks ticking every step of the way, the design is digitized and bounced off a satellite to a print shop in Hong Kong where the bits are reconverted to atoms, arranged as black patterns on white paper. The package of printed invitations is rushed to the Hong Kong airport and loaded onto a jet. Later that week, the artist picks up the finished job back on Main Street. This everyday task required the organization of hundreds of people. It's the way we live now.

But though society has never been so organized and we know our lives are deeply entangled with other people's lives, we have never been more isolated in private agendas and personal schedules. We rush to appointments and meetings, bumping others on their way to other appointments and meetings. Time, it seems, has become the scarcest of resources. Thirty seconds of "gray-bar time"—waiting for a computer program to finish—can seem much too long. Each of us now has our own clock strapped to our arms or constantly blinking on our cell phones, and we rush through the week on time without a village tower in sight. Time, the very stuff of life, seems to be running out.

For the most part, we did not shape the systems that now shape us. We don't even know for sure who did shape them or what they are really up to. Because commerce has made the most visible and spectacular use of modern organization, we understand that a lot of what is happening is because someone is making money. Though this may not be bad, enriching someone else is hardly a goal that brings people together. But we keep moving, trying to put aside a little something for ourselves. Time is money.

The world is moving faster and faster and change is the name of the game, manic consultants keep asserting. We need to forget faster and faster, just to make room for the new. Who remembers DOS keystroke commands?

At a town meeting I was invited to not long ago, the school superintendent became quite animated, talking about the pressures that rapid change puts upon schools. His voice getting urgent, he cited statistics

and painted a picture in which we were all going to become obsoles-
cent if we didn't do something. Our students were not prepared for the
world that was rapidly forming around us. It was nearing crisis. His
training and his inbox made keeping up with the times seem urgent. I
wondered whether that training had given him the perspective to dis-
tinguish between a fad and a trend. I wondered whether it had helped
him develop the skill to set priorities wisely.

Out loud I suggested that if things were changing too rapidly for
schools to keep up, maybe more time should be spent studying things
that changed very slowly, if they changed at all.

He looked genuinely perplexed. "What things?" he asked.

Running a school is not all that different from playing a video game.
Keep your eyes on the screen. Keep moving. Last year it was community service. Then it was school-to-work. React. Hurry. We need to
change. One effect of such leadership is a kind of self-inflicted demen-
tia. I worked in a school that was similar to a person with Alzheimer's,
unable to remember from moment to moment what it was doing, what
remained to be done, or even who its friends were. We began lots of
things but finished nothing. The bookshelves in the administrative offices were laden with unread binders, all that was left of abandoned
projects that not so long ago had been touted as solutions to our problems.

Teachers were accustomed to being corralled and given handouts,
but they knew there would be no follow-through. Next year they would
be on to something different. They would efficiently forget all this.
They sat politely but they no longer really listened.

When I was studying to become an English teacher at the beginning
of my career, one of the books I was given to read was *The Educated
Imagination*, first published in 1964 by Canadian literary critic
Northrop Frye. Near the end of that book, Frye says that "the society
around us looks like the real world, but . . . there's a great deal of illusion in it, the kind of illusion that propaganda and slanted news and
prejudice and a great deal of advertising appeal to . . . It changes very
rapidly, and people who don't know of any other world can never understand what makes it change."

Might not this have been written this morning? Frye goes on to argue that the real world is not changing. "The real world," he says, "is

the world of what humanity has done, and therefore can do, the world revealed to us in the arts and sciences. This is the world that won't go away, the world out of which we built the Canada of 1942, are now building the Canada of 1962, and will be building the quite different Canada of 1982."

The real world, like gravity, may be invisible. We do not see it but we see its effects. The best education is about learning to apprehend, behind those effects, the things that do not change: the timeless patterns and the eternal forces. These are things that educators, even school superintendents, might usefully ponder, if they can find the time.

THE ART OF SLOW THINKING

The most powerful education is not driven by markets or election cycles. Instead, it aims at passing on cultural knowledge that has taken centuries to acquire and that will remain useful even after our business partners change and our transportation systems are reinvented. It's okay that cultural mores and institutional practices change more slowly than markets. That's their job.

"Don't hurry," should be the motto inscribed over every schoolroom door. But also, "Don't stop. Don't waste time." Schools should be caretakers of slow knowledge, also called wisdom.

Every good school needs some teachers who are less interested in high-velocity markets and the shifting priorities of political cycles than in passing on the techniques of intelligence—such things as how to evaluate evidence, how to use math to perceive patterns too large or too small for direct observation, what it takes to develop friendships and alliances, how to organize a town and hold it together, how fights begin and how they end, how justice comes into the world and how it perishes, how to discern between things ephemeral and things of permanent worth, what it feels like to win a kingdom but lose your soul, and so on.

Change, of course, is assured—indeed, it is irrepressible. But the more things change, the more important it becomes that we learn to see what does not change, or changes only slowly. We need to know what is solid ground. We need firm footing to wrestle with what comes.

Familiarity with the past more than anything else provides us with that footing. In times of rapid change the institutions we most need to strengthen are those that preserve memory. The most reliable way to know something of the future is to know the past. The longer our memories, the longer our view of the future.

In *The Clock of the Long Now*, Stewart Brand (2000) reports that in 1980 the Swedish navy received a letter from the Forestry Department announcing that the ship lumber that had been requested was ready. In 1829, the Swedish Parliament had ordered twenty thousand trees planted on Visingsö, in the lake Vätern. It took 150 years for an oak to mature and they anticipated a shortage of ship lumber during the 1990s. The move had been opposed by the bishop of Strängnäs because he didn't believe people would still have wars by then and even if they did, ships would probably no longer be made of wood. Parliament overrode him. They got the details wrong, but by thinking in the long term they did the right thing anyway. The worth of that mature oak forest today is beyond calculation.

Wisdom occurs more often among older people because they have had to live with more consequences of bad choices. As people see and understand longer time frames, their thinking gets stronger and their decision making gets better. Institutions that think in longer time frames also tend to be less foolish. Companies that rely on repeat customers tend to be more honest and fair than those who believe that tomorrow will always be a brand-new game.

Schools today need institutional practices and institutional goals that organize their daily labors around visions longer than a fifty-minute period, longer than a semester, longer than a superintendent's tenure, longer than this political cycle's hot problem, and longer even than a teacher's career. It may be helpful to think about what James P. Carse (1986), religion professor at New York University, calls "the infinite game." He says, "a finite game is played for the purpose of winning, an infinite game for the purpose of continuing the game." Football is a finite game. Gardening is an infinite game. A political campaign is a finite game. A family is an infinite game. A business deal is a finite game. A religion is an infinite game.

Charles Hampden-Turner and Fons Trompenaars (1997) built upon Carse's thought. In a finite game, they point out, winners exclude losers. In an infinite game, winners teach losers better plays. In a finite game, the winner takes all. In an infinite game, winning is widely shared. In a finite game, the players' aims are identical. In an infinite game, the players' aims are diverse. In a finite game, rules are fixed in advance to guarantee a single winner. In an infinite game, rules are changed along the way by agreement. In a finite game, energy is focused in short-term, decisive contests. In an infinite game, energy is invested in the long-term. Finite games focus on how they end. Infinite games focus on how they continue.

Good schools, like good communities, good economies, and good families, are playing an infinite game. They may include finite games within them, but they ensure that these games don't displace the larger play or corrupt it. James Carse ends his book with a statement that bears further reflection: "There is but one infinite game."

LIVING THE INFINITE GAME

I have some thoughts about the infinite game and how it should be played. So do you. Here are the basics: it includes everybody, it involves all knowledge, and it includes all of the past and all of the future. That's quite a bit. So where do we start?

We start with particular places—the ones that are accessible to us. Place is the intersection of nature and history and culture. It is the tangible locality that roots our abstract and conceptual understandings in reality. It is the first thing we know of the world. It is a reference we share that allows us to think and feel together. It is the setting of the experiences that matter to us most and make us human. It is all we know of the world.

And we start with our families. Family, suggests historian Elliott West, is the tool that can help students connect all the disconnections of time and place they face in the modern world. In a speech to the Montana Heritage Project, he pointed out that "families intertwine the chaotic details of every past time and bind them with the present and with us. For those of us interested in how societies have worked, families have always been the center of ordinary human lives. Their greatest power is to implicate you and me in the emotional world of real people who have come and gone, people we will join soon enough."

He suggested that we study the past using our own families as a point of entry, and as a linking principle. Doing family history research is not primarily about creating pedigree charts. Rather, it is about understanding the human experience. More people than ever are connecting not only with their distant ancestors, reimagining the worlds they knew and pondering what they faced and how their world grew into our world, they are also connecting with like-minded people around the world.

Through a focus on family history research, students can be drawn to oral history, which involves reading, writing, speaking, listening, summarizing, and analyzing as well as the fundamental work of turning toward elders with interest and compassion. They can be drawn to primary document research, which includes making a research plan, using finding aids, writing letters, evaluating conflicting evidence, and synthesizing original conclusions. They can be drawn to published texts that treat historical periods, specific events, political history, personal experience, and the rest of the human record.

They can join the worldwide effort of others who are trying to understand the world through the work of reconstructing their family history. They can discover what has been lost. They can contribute important information to the shared work. That woman in Ireland who is looking for an uncle who was last heard from somewhere in Montana in 1875—how is she to find what happened to him? The answer may lie on a gravestone in that cemetery just up the hill from where you live. If that Irish woman had the name and the date on that gravestone, she could find an obituary, and if she had the obituary, she might have the name of employers and information about historical events that touched his life. One thing leads to another and to another and, given time, to all things.

Right now there is work to do. Cemetery records and courthouse records of real estate transactions and marriages are all being put online. Students who share this work will learn to organize information, to create and maintain databases, to research and write, and to place a value upon the human record. And though we start with familiar places and with our own families, we don't stop there. Family history leads to community history, and community history leads to national and world history and history includes all other disciplines. As schools, in partnerships with museums and historical societies, begin to maintain community archives containing research done by students and other community members, these archives will become the most important institution in the school.

If you would like to test the educational value of such materials, you can conduct a simple test. Set up two tables in a classroom. On one table, put the most seductive materials you can locate from the large publishers of educational materials, with their four-color illustrations and lavish layouts. On the other table place some old photographs of the local neighborhood, a few old maps of the place, and a collection of old newspapers. Bring some kids into the room and watch where they go and what they do. Be ready to be quiet for a while, because the students will not hear you. They'll be buzzing with excitement, pointing things out to one another. They'll be engaged.

A good local archive will include long-term ecological studies, local geography, studies of transportation systems and public utilities and studies of local folkways and traditions. Caring for such a collection of local research and adding to it will be everyone's responsibility. And the work that is done in such schools will not be ephemera. It is intended to last forever.

Schools that act as catalysts for this work will find support coming from unexpected directions. They will have occasions to take delight in seeing students experiencing moments of pure motivation, teachers feeling oddly revitalized, and communities coming sporadically to life, reengaging the schools.

JOINED IN TIME

The collection will not seem grand at first. The first year it might have only fourteen biographical essays done by a senior English class. But fourteen essays is something, if it is kept. In ten years, the value will be clearer. Some of the work will be in file folders, awaiting the right researcher to take it further. Some work will be published documents that hold in place organized bodies of work that have been done. And some work will be ready for publication online. Since the work is intended to last forever, it is not done in undue haste.

When there are hundreds of documents, teachers who had shown no interest at the beginning will begin to pay attention. Nearly every student in their classes will be able to find information on their own families. This will provoke further questions.

In twenty years, everyone will understand the value of what is being done. The archives will be quite large and everybody will have a personal interest in some part of it. Community members will come to the school to do their own research alongside students. Eventually, it will be understood as the school's most important educational resource, allowing learners to move beyond mass schooling toward learning engagements with the real world, the only place it actually exists, which is locally. Using and adding to this community research project can clarify and deepen the school's central purpose, and the collection itself orients new teachers and new students to the larger mission of which they are a part. That mission is simply to use learning to make the world a better place, starting here, the only place we will ever be.

In doing the work, students will come to understand more of what it has meant and now means to be human. They will see the world from more of its perspectives: that of victors, that of the defeated, that of women, that of kings, that of slaves. They might be brought to ponder the way consequences follow actions, not always quickly and not always fairly. They might meditate on justice. They might learn new songs.

Elliott West reminded us that "all of us sleep with ghosts." From them, we can "learn about the world they knew, and how it grew into ours." Even more important, by inviting them into our lives, "we resurrect our humanness."

In fifty years, people will have a hard time imagining a school without archives. A school without archives would be—well, a place full of busywork, a place where time is a burden, and people watch the clock and wait, a place where nothing that is done is real or permanent, a place where people think mostly about token rewards and cliques, a place where people are bored and restless and angry—a place where people waste the very essence of their lives: time.

CHAPTER 10

A Hunger for Reality

"The heritage project is not just a class—it's an adventure!" said Kelsey Miller, a high school senior in Harlowton, Montana. She and her fellow seniors in teacher Nancy Widdicombe's English class made the Bair family ranch in their hometown the subject of scholarly research, tracing across generations the one-hundred-year rise of one of the largest sheep operations in the nation.

Drawing on interviews, research in bank and museum archives, and documentation of ranching culture today, the students published their work in a book that adds significant detail to the history of Montana and of their community. Through a multimedia presentation, they shared the story of their research quest with their community at a special Heritage Evening attended by more than a hundred people.

These students took their schoolwork seriously in part because the adults took it seriously. Though most schoolwork is ephemera or busywork, thrown away as soon as it is graded, the work of Kelsey and her fellow students is preserved at the Montana State Historical Society archives as a resource for future researchers.

Thousands of students in thirty-one Montana communities have participated in the Montana Heritage Project. The projects vary greatly, but what they have in common is that students are guided through a cycle of inquiry, summarized in the ALERT processes: Ask important questions; Listen to the historical record as it exists in libraries and archives; Explore beyond the library by conducting interviews, visiting sites and events, and creating a detailed history of the present; Reflect on what has been learned and how it fits with or changes existing knowledge;

and Teach the story of what has been learned by creating gifts of scholarship that can be given back to the community.

The model is simple and flexible, because the real power of heritage projects flows not from a method or a technique so much as from faith in people—both kids and elders—and a commitment to act on that faith by inviting others to join the work.

One important work people in any community can share is that of gathering, documenting, preserving, and presenting the cultural and natural heritage of their families and the local places they know. We will never have enough professional scholars to do this work, and if local people don't do it, it won't get done. This realization is easy to communicate to young people, so they know we aren't being patronizing when we tell them they have real and important work to do.

At each stage in the process, adult community members are invited to join the work as mentors, coresearchers, and guides, so students are engaged in a comprehensive learning model while community members are invited to help document and research their own lives, telling their stories in their own way.

For more than a decade, I've visited communities doing heritage projects, and the reasons people both young and old are drawn to community-centered education have become increasingly clear. People sense the loss of community, and in the troubles that follow such loss, they are looking for ways to restore what they know they need. The only way we can meet the long list of adolescent "needs" that researchers have identified in our nation's high schools is to revitalize our communities. Sometimes, by trying to meet every adolescent need by developing a special program dedicated to it, we've inadvertently undermined the power of community. It becomes second nature to think that "they" should do something, when quite often only "we" can get it done. The greatest risks to "at-risk" adolescents emanate from the absence of strong communities. Adolescents live on the threshold between family and the larger community, trying to construct identities that, inevitably, have narrative structures, and substantial research indicates that when the various adult groups that surround teenagers—parents, teachers, employers, church leaders, community leaders—tell coherent stories about the things worth wanting and the right ways to get them—teens make the transition from youth to adulthood quite smoothly.

On the other hand, when those groups lose faith with one another and tell conflicting stories many young people get lost, causing tremendous pain to themselves, their families, and their communities. One of the most vivid signs of failed community is our large population of troubled youth. As our schools have become larger and more distant from their communities so that teachers and neighborhood adults inhabit different realities, the effectiveness of schools, especially for troubled youth, plummets.

Inviting community members to help with heritage projects brings the power of community to bear on teaching. For those coming of age, which is largely a process of weaving one's individual story into the tapestry of community, a neighborhood's folkways may be more powerful educative forces than the school's formal curricula, for good or ill. This is why serious educators are turning their attention to community-centered teaching, looking for ways to reconnect schools and communities. Teachers in the Montana Heritage Project demonstrate that schools can build or rebuild relationships between young people and their communities simply by establishing projects that get the young and old working together.

Teachers remain true to their academic mission by focusing such projects on inquiry into the community itself: the defining events and persons of the past, its relationship to the natural environment, its place in national and world events, its current challenges, and its future prospects.

Renee Rasmussen's students in Chester write a regular local history column for the community newspaper. Phil Leonardi's freshmen geography classes partnered with the U.S. Forest Service to research how the community of Corvallis has been affected through the decades by forest fires. Jerry Girard's Montana history class in Dillon compiled a history of Beaverhead County's rural one- and two-room schools. Students created a map showing the location of each past and present school in the county as well as a detailed time line of educational events in the county from 1863 to the present. This was the basis for a permanent exhibit at the Beaverhead County Museum, featuring video interviews with students and teachers from the past and present.

Darlene Beck's English class in Townsend completed an eighty-five year history of Broadwater High School. Students used local newspaper archives, courthouse records, school yearbooks dating from 1916 to the present, and the archives of the Broadwater Historical Society and Museum for background research. They conducted interviews with former students, teachers, principals, clerks, and board members, and produced a slide show for parent conferences and a book that was placed in the local museum and library. Students in Nancy Heggen's classes in White Sulphur Springs used courthouse records and oral histories to write the first history of the county's early twentieth-century poor farm, putting it in the context of strategies for dealing with the poor throughout European and American history.

Many teachers have participated in the Veterans History Project, sponsored by the Library of Congress. This program gives high schools the chance to act as partners with the library. It has been a powerful motivator for both students and veterans, and the supporting resources that embed professional oral history standards in materials can be used in the classroom. In Bigfork, Mary Sullivan's juniors gathered vivid stories from World War II, Korean, Vietnam, and Gulf war veterans. They borrowed photographs from the veterans, scanned them, and incorporated them with narratives drawn from oral histories into a multimedia presentation, which was shown to a standing-room only crowd at the 435-seat Bigfork Center for the Performing Arts.

The Library of Congress's leadership through the Veterans History Project and the Montana Heritage Project in organizing serious scholarly work that can be accomplished with the help of students establishes a model that other cultural institutions should follow. Across the state, students have been participating in the Veterans History Project sponsored by the Library of Congress in cooperation with the Montana Heritage Project. The materials gathered and created through the projects are preserved for posterity by the Library of Congress. Students are given the opportunity to work as associates with the library, and teachers are provided high-quality teaching materials.

The Veterans History Project is important for several reasons. For one thing, the stories our veterans have to tell are important. On this there is unusually widespread agreement, and the bill to fund the project passed the U.S. Congress with no opposition. But there are other things to think about as well. The Library of Congress models an important direction for American education: authentic research projects sponsored by cultural and scientific agencies, in which agencies with deep expertise design projects and materials for schools, embedding educational standards in real work while providing scaffolding to help students and teachers meet challenging criteria.

The development of educational standards has been an important exercise in clarifying what students need to know and be able to do. Now we need to teach those standards through exciting projects. It's time to get past lists of things to teach and to develop high-quality teaching strategies, embedding those standards in real work that allows learners to investigate rich and challenging issues in the real world. Student work should culminate in public exhibitions that provide both accountability and a chance for students to contribute gifts of scholarship to their communities.

What schools need today are research opportunities that allow them to practice advanced skills while working with the scaffolding provided by specialists. The Library of Congress is one leader but there are others. The Long-Term Ecological Network (LTER), a program of the National Science Foundation, recognizes that high school students can contribute to cutting edge scientific research and that the collaboration between scientists and students can benefit both.

Scientists at the LTER's Cedar Creek facility in Minnesota challenge other scientists "to think of ways in which [students can] collect data of interest beyond the confines of the school, either as part of a larger network, or addressing questions from a broader perspective by providing data useful in addressing state-of-the-art scientific questions."

As we develop collaborative projects between schools and other agencies, several things can happen. First, students become better educated through working with artists, historians, business leaders, scientists, and others on authentic projects in the real world. Tough standards are more likely to be met when it's clear that such standards aren't merely more of the mysterious impositions that bureaucracies routinely emit, like a ban on bottles of mouthwash on airlines, but that instead they grow out of real world concerns. Writing is good not because the teacher says so, but because it organizes accurate information and communicates it clearly, precisely, and accurately.

Second, we reconnect with the social basis of learning. Hard learning is most often accomplished in teams that allow communication

about what, exactly, needs to be done and what various bits of information actually mean. Social learning is much easier to organize and
monitor now that we have blogs, wikis, and discussion boards. Students and teachers have reasons to use the technological tools that link
them to each other at the same time local teams are linked to state and
national projects. They become skilled at using websites that include
artwork, databases, audio and video files, and writing.

Third, we inject civic discourse, service learning, and character education into the heart of our academic instruction. The habits of scholarship and of civic discourse—carefulness, curiosity, honesty, patience,
and openness to new perspectives—come alive by being enacted by
living communities. What do we do when everything we've tried has
failed? Chennell Brewer, a high school senior, was working on a group
research project into the history of the Poor Farm in White Sulphur
Springs when she came across some odd entries in the Poor Farm Register at the county courthouse. In her research report, she noted that
"Walter Young, Harley Gay, and John Fadock were all admitted to the
Poor Farm on September 23, 1916. The three men had arrived in the
county on September 13 and 19 and had similar injuries. Young and
Gay were found to have bullet wounds and Fadock had a wound from
a club. Young died the day after he was admitted and Fadock and Gay
were discharged on September 30, 1916." She decided to find out the
rest of the story.

But things weren't easy. In fact, it came to seem impossible. "At the
local courthouse I dug through the aged Poor Farm Register, Registers
of Prisoners Confined, Sheriff's Day Book, coroner's reports, judge's
docket, judge's reports, local newspapers, local cemetery records and
many other archives," Chennell said. But she found nary a mention of
the men or of what had happened. Her research was a complete bust. It
was not, however, a waste of time. Chennell's teacher, Nancy Heggen,
was able to model perseverance, ingenuity, diligence, and thorough-
ness, which are vital to learn but hard to teach through traditional
school assignments.

And then there's the taste for adventure and openness to serendipity
that are vital to most high-level accomplishment. The next year, in a
different heritage project, Chennell and her class were researching a
1916 train holdup that occurred in the town. An old newspaper report

mentioned that an earlier holdup had occurred twelve days before. There had been a shootout in which fifty-some shots were fired and several people were injured. Three of those people suffered familiar injuries: two bullet wounds (one fatal) and a club wound. The date of the train robbery was one day before the date the three men were admitted to the poor farm. With this new lead, Chennell expanded her search to newspapers throughout the region, watching for details about the September incident.

Here's an excerpt of Chennell's report:

I found many articles containing information about the hold up. From the information gathered, I was able to piece together an outline of the story although the details were still somewhat sketchy. That soon changed.

The entire P.A.D. class took a February field trip to the Montana Historical Society in Helena. My classmate Jason Barker and I sat down in front of the microfilm readers and began reading newspapers. We read the *Judith Gap Journal, Helena Independent, Montana Record, Great Falls Daily Tribune*, and *Lewistown News Argus* for the dates September 20–26, 1916. Jason and I copied six newspaper articles to take back to school.

I collected eighteen newspaper articles that helped to fill in a lot of details. I was able to come up with a relatively solid account of, and the possible reasoning behind, the September train brawl.

During the latter months of 1916, railroad workers, many of whom were members of the Industrial Workers of the World union (I.W.W.), were pushing for change. According to the *Judith Gap Journal*, the workers were "an idealistic organization of unskilled laborers" who were "endeavoring to better working conditions."

In September, the eight-hour day, established by the Adamson law, was accepted by railroad workers. The law allowed workers to receive the same pay for an eight-hour workday that they had been receiving for nine or ten hours of work. There was abundant controversy between railroad magnates and railway workers over the effects of this law. The magnates claimed the new policy would have a significantly detrimental effect on profits, and the workers cried poverty due to low pay and higher costs of living.

The debate became more heated when the "railroad executives advisory committee, representing the railroads affected by the Adamson eight-hour law," began an investigation to "ascertain, if possible, the effect of the law, as to practical operating problems," and also the law's legality. This decision, no doubt, riled many railroad workers, as well as members of the general public. The gun battle that broke out on the afternoon of September 22, 1916, at the railway yards of the Milwaukee Railroad in Judith Gap, was likely a product of the "eight-hour" hullabaloo.

On that September afternoon, around thirty members of the I.W.W.—Wobblies—attempted to take control of a Great Northern freight train in Judith Gap. These thirty were part of the same gang that attacked a Great Northern train near Havre, Montana just a few days earlier and escaped. The outcome in Judith Gap was a little different, though.

The gang met resistance from the Gap's train crew, and shots soon rang throughout the railway yards. At the sound of gunshots, citizens of Judith Gap rushed to the yards, nearly all of them armed. The citizens joined in the fray, aiding the train crew. Fifty shots and many wounds later, the citizens of Judith Gap succeeded in rounding up most of the villains.

Approximately twenty of the offenders were jailed, although the leader, who was the first to fire shots, escaped. He supposedly notified several fellow Wobblies to attack and free the twenty who were jailed. However, word of his plan got out, so Deputy Sheriff Rice kept a number of armed men at the jail where the prisoners were being held. Nothing ever came of the supposed Wobbly posse.

Out of the many wounds sustained by people during the melee, three were reported heavily in newspapers. They were the wounds of Harley Gay, Walter Young and an unnamed man that—perhaps not coincidentally—had the exact wounds of John Fadock. Walter was an I.W.W. union member. He was shot in the hip and the bullet continued through his abdomen. He was admitted to the Poor Farm in White Sulphur Springs on September 23, 1916, a day after the train battle. Walter died the following day and is rumored to be buried in the White Sulphur Springs cemetery.

Harley was sixteen years old and also a union member. He was admitted to the Poor Farm for a bullet wound in the leg, a wound received in the gun battle at Judith Gap, according to the *Judith Gap Journal* and *Great Falls Daily Tribune*. Harley testified that the gang of troublesome Wobblies forced him to travel with them. However, I found no confirmation of this statement. Harley was discharged from the Poor Farm a week after his admittance.

John Fadock's name never appeared in any newspaper articles, but there are numerous mentions of a man that received a club wound from a brake stick in the *Judith Gap Journal* and *Great Falls Daily Tribune*. John was admitted to the Poor Farm the same day as Walter and Harley for, according to the Poor Farm Register, a "wound from a club." I believe that Fadock was the man the newspapers were referring to.

John had been making a run for cover when he was clubbed with the brake stick. The stick became a weapon when Brakeman Kenneth Hay was no longer able to defend his brake position from the pistol-waving rioters. Hay was shot. His injury wasn't serious but it was serious enough to put him out of the action.

Twenty Wobblies were rounded up by a posse of local citizens and jailed in Judith Gap to await the arrival of Sheriff Nagues who would escort them to the Meagher County jail in White Sulphur Springs. A hearing for the I.W.W. troublemakers was held on September 25, 1916 in White Sulphur Springs. Most of the rioters were not charged and were released. Three of them, however, were charged with assault: Max Muller, Fred Christensen and George Flier. Because it was unknown whose shots actually did damage, and because the I.W.W. provoked the riot, the assault charges were the only ones pushed in court.

According to the *Judith Gap Journal*, the three Wobblies held in jail were working their hardest to have the train incident investigated by Congress, which had previously investigated a riot in Everett, Washington, that involved the I.W.W. and local citizens. The three convicted rioters held in the Meagher County jail thought they might benefit from a similar congressional investigation. However, the paper reported that the likelihood of help from an investigation "would be extremely slim for the three convicts."

The jailbirds' attorney, Samuel Block from Chicago, mounted a vigorous defense, but in spite of this, the three were found guilty of assault on January 18, 1917, four months after the fray at Judith Gap. Muller was sentenced to three to four years plus the six months he served in the county jail, and Christensen received a similar three to four year sentence. Flier came out the worst. He was the only one proven to have shot anyone—the brakeman, Kenneth Hay—so he received a harsher punishment of four to five years.

I was relieved to have completed my investigation into the three mystery men. I thought back to last year which was an exercise in frustration. Even though several people assisted me with my research and even though I had access to hundreds of different documents and records, I could not find any information about the men other than that they were admitted to the Poor Farm and left in one way or another. I ended the year with a few tantalizing facts to show for not only my efforts, but the efforts of Ms. Heggen and several community members.

At the beginning of her quest, the world of trains, Wobblies, and poor farms was nearly as distant and exotic to Chennell as stories of medieval knights. But she now knows quite a lot about the beginning decades of the twentieth century, and, more important, about how historical knowledge is pieced together from primary sources and reasonable conjecture. With tremendous help from long-time staff members at the Montana Historical Society, Marcella Sherfy and Dave Walter, Chennell made huge progress toward understanding, more profoundly than is often the case for high school students, what knowledge actually is. She was engaged in research and writing. Her identity increasingly included the story of herself as a person who uses academic tools to figure things out.

Students in the Montana Heritage Project have assisted professional writers in doing historical research, worked under the supervision of natural resource agencies and museums, and completed hundreds of oral history projects for the Library of Congress. In the past, a person often needed to get to graduate school before being allowed to work in an apprentice mode with skilled researchers. This has been an enormous waste. High school students and undergraduates have been consigned to rather stupid "research" assignments that involved moving secondary source information from one place to another, adding nothing, while all around them agencies wander on in the dark, without the resources to construct and organize knowledge that would have been invaluable. Both society and individual students are better served when high school students research and write the history of local churches and businesses, do market surveys for local planners, gather information about local shopping habits for the chamber of commerce, and update lists of species found along a local creek, not to mention contribute to state and regional data bases of bird sightings, meteorological readings, water and air quality indicators, archaeological surveys, and hundreds of similar research projects. It's more fun for teachers, too. "I don't like busy work any more than the students do," said Corvallis teacher Annemarie Kanenwisher. "I'd rather do the real work, too."

We can now see in broad outline one of the visions that will drive schooling in the twenty-first century. It is slowly sinking in how dramatically tools such as Google can change everything about schooling, and emancipatory lessons from thousands of homeschoolers are slowly penetrating the dense protective shells of bureaucratic habit. The digital age leads to the learning age, and we will create a framework for the shared pursuit of knowledge that includes local schools and communities, scientific and cultural organizations, universities, government agencies, and families. Schooling, like the rest of life, becomes a series of learning projects.

We now have the tools. The kids are ready. We are surrounded by opportunity. Since 1995, several hundred such projects have been completed in many Montana towns. By attempting original research of lasting value, teachers reverse the tendency of schools to turn in on themselves, allowing routines and habits to fill up the days.

People who live in communities that work know that in addition to the exchange economy they also need a vibrant gift economy. In spite of the beauty and efficiency of well-regulated markets, there remain important things that should never be for sale and other important things that should be available to anyone, regardless of their ability to pay. Montana Heritage Project teachers understand community as a self-sustained state of grace where we do not—cannot—earn everything we get. We don't earn the moments of sunshine catching the faces of friends as we are on our way to accomplish some purpose that pulls us together. We do not earn the rain that falls on the wicked and just alike. In good towns and neighborhoods, people understand this state of grace and teach it to their children. Schools can best teach it by taking seriously the unique mission of formal education, taking seriously the ideals of scholarship, and leading students not to copy-and-paste research but to the real thing, original work with primary sources. Young people in need of identities are in fact young poets in need of stories. A good community is a repository of just the stories they need.

To adolescents, reality is new terrain. Like country folk newly arrived in a strange city, their fortunes depend on their learning well what sort of place surrounds them. What are the rules? What does the start of trouble look like? What should be avoided and what should not be missed? What are the marvels? What is the extent of possibility and where are the limits? A fortunate traveler might find a long-term resident with a penchant for stories—an old hand willing to show the ropes. For teenagers new to this world, gathering and writing the stories of local and family history is a near-perfect introduction to the place where of necessity they must find themselves.

Because reality is fabulous, true stories are often more profound than those the students would have made up. Those of us who have read lots of "creative" writing by young people know how banal it tends to be. Their time might have been better spent grappling with the surprising and anomalous stuff of actual lives in actual places. We can help young minds work the crucial transformation from primary school fantasies to the reality-based dreams of young adulthood by examining and pondering things as they really have been and things as they really are. Of course, this is seldom a simple thing—sorting through facts to see how things really are. Done well, the process helps us see the strangeness of our plight, the way that our consciousness cocreates reality, so that for us what is real is always partly imagined and partly unimagined. We are creatures of passions whose real landscapes are always partly dreamed. We are neither victims nor gods, but actors in realms we can partly revise. Seeing this, we begin to see the true power of imagination, which has everything to do with the storied structure of reality.

In researching the role of music during the Great Depression in the lives of people in her hometown of Libby, high school senior Rachel Reckin came across George Neills, the businessman who built the sawmill that provided the town's economic lifeblood for decades. Among other things, she learned that during the startup phase early in the twentieth century, although success was not assured and careful stewardship of money seemed vital, Neills ignored his father's counsel and spent a small fortune buying a good piano and having it shipped to the small town surrounded by mountains in western Montana. Reading his letters at the local museum, she saw in his character a connection between that willful choice to have music in spite of the risk to the bottom line and his later decision to keep his mill operating at a loss through the Depression so that people didn't lose their paychecks. She made a personal connection when she learned that the piano she had heard at church every Sunday while growing up had been a gift from him. She even found in an obscure letter the historical detail that was a perfect ending for her essay. In later life, Neills needed an operation to insert a pin into his shoulder. After the operation, he would have a limited range of motion. The surgeon said he would need to decide once and for all the angle of his shoulder. So he had the surgeon take measurements while he sat at his piano and played. "Put it right there," he said, looking out the window beyond the mountains and sky.

The stories that George Neills lived became a gift to Libby, and, decades after his death, to a young researcher looking for things of interest in dusty archives. The story that Rachel wrote became a fresh gift to the town, where few people remembered Neills. The audience for research-based nonfiction about local history is far greater than the audience for fiction penned by seventeen-year-olds. We escaped the Dark Ages by organizing the pursuit of knowledge within a gift economy, and every generation holds the Dark Ages at bay through the same processes. It's only a story, but a story coming true.

Guests at Youth Heritage Festival sponsored by the Montana Heritage Project often comment on the enthusiasm of the young people. It's hard to be pessimistic at these events. Gathered at an academic conference to read their research and to hear the research of others, the students speak with passion about the importance of their work. It's fun—that feeling of having joined a new community, the community of scholars.

All communities are always facing trouble. It's quite inevitable that we are always confronted with some need to understand better some social, environmental, political, economic, or moral shift around us. A glance at newspaper headlines makes it clear that challenges lie in all directions. In a good high school, these real challenges can drive a good part of the curriculum. We can teach much of what we need to teach by beginning with the real questions we face. As we do, young people understand that they have allies in many of the problems before them—elders who share their plight. By beginning with real questions, we slip free of the abstractions that have led so many intellectuals astray. We don't really learn about community—or other trendy abstractions, such as tolerance, diversity, and cooperation—by hearing them preached and seeing posters in the hall. We learn about them by engaging in practices that give us working knowledge of where the ideals come from and why they sometimes matter and how they often fail. When classes are organized into research teams working with community members and organizations to form questions and make answers, community ceases being a buzzword in a mission statement and becomes a way of life. In good communities, adults build council fires and think together. And it is concern about their children, more than anything, that calls them together.

In education-centered communities, school is a busy place. One group of students is working with a handful of community mentors on a new museum display, telling the story of how the community responded to the floods of 1964 for the annual community heritage festival in the spring. The heritage festival is the most important event at the school each year, attracting larger audiences than basketball games. Another group is finishing up the transcriptions of interviews with residents at the local rest home, to add to the local library's collection of biographies of people who lived in the town. The sophomores have responsibility for systematically interviewing the community's elders, with the long-range goal of having available biographies of everyone who ever lived in the town. Fifth graders are editing the photos they took at specific reference points through the valley, where every year the fifth-grade classes return to take new photographs, creating a visual record of changes in the ecosystems and the built environment. The juniors are organizing a large-scale study of the history of transportation in the valley, from the time of Indian trails to the latest highway bridge. Much of their research is being done in microfilm of the area's newspapers. The scholars at Alexandria would recognize this place.

Young people are drawn to the adventure. They wake up and come to the fire. They join the conversation, aroused by the power of the real.

References

Anderson, E. (1990). *Streetwise*. Chicago: University of Chicago Press.

Argyris, C., and Schön, D. (1974). *Theory in practice: Increasing professional effectiveness*. San Francisco: Jossey-Bass.

Basso, K. H. (1986). Stalking with stories: Names, places, and moral narratives among the Western Apache. *Antaeus 57*, 112.

Beery, R., and Schug, M. C. (1984). Young people and community. *National Council for the Social Studies, Bulletin No. 73*.

Bellah, R. N., Madsen, R., Sullivan, W. M., Swidler, A., and Tipton, S. M. (1991). *The good society*. New York: Vintage.

Berry, W. (1989). Discipline and hope. In *A continuous harmony: Essays cultural and agricultural*, 83–162. Fort Washington, PA: Harvest Books.

———. (1990). *What are people for?* San Francisco: North Point Press.

Bishop, J. (1985, Summer). Game of freeze out: Marguerite Greenfield and her battle with the Great Northern Railway, 1920–1929. *Montana the Magazine of Western History*, 14–27.

Brand, S. (2000). *The clock of the long now: Time and responsibility*. New York: Basic.

Calne, D. B. (2001). *Within reason: Rationality and human behavior*. New York: Knopf.

Carse, J. P. (1986). *Finite and infinite games: A vision of life as play and possibility*. New York: Ballantine.

Cheff Sr., B. (1994). *Indian trails and grizzly tales*. Stevensville, MT: Stoneydale Press.

Commission on Children at Risk (2003). *Hardwired to connect: The new scientific case for authoritative communities*. New York: Institute for American Values.

Theobald, P., and Curtiss, J. (2000, Spring). Communities as Curricula. *Forum for Applied Research and Public Policy 15* (1), 106.

Vygotsky, L. S. (1988). *Mind in society: The development of higher psychological processes*. Cambridge, MA: Harvard University Press.

Weberman, D. (1997, June). The nonfixity of the historical past. *The Review of Metaphysics 50* (4), 749.

White, R. (1991). *"It's your misfortune and none of my own": A new history of the American West*. Norman: University of Oklahoma Press.

Wollaston, P. (1997). *Homesteading: A Montana family album*. New York: Lyons Press.